CONTENTS

Housing and Anti-Poverty Strategies: A Good Practice Guide

Tim Brown and Jon Passmore

Chartered Institute of Housing
Joseph Rowntree Foundation

The Chartered Institute of Housing
The Chartered Institute of Housing is the professional organisation for all people who work in housing. Its purpose is to take a strategic and leading role in encouraging and promoting the provision of good quality affordable housing for all. The Institute has more than 14,000 members working in local authorities, housing associations and other social landlords, the private sector and educational institutions.

The Joseph Rowntree Foundation
The Joseph Rowntree Foundation has supported this publication as part of its programme of research and innovative development projects, which it hopes will be of value to policy makers and practitioners. The facts presented and views expressed, however, are those of the authors and not necessarily those of the Foundation.

Housing and Anti-Poverty Strategies: A Good Practice Guide
Prepared by Tim Brown, De Montfort University and Jon Passmore, Taff Housing Association

Commissioning Editor: Ross Fraser, Director of Professional Practice, Chartered Institute of Housing

Editor: Tony Trott

Published by the Chartered Institute of Housing and the Joseph Rowntree Foundation

ISBN 1 900396 01 7

Graphic design by Jeremy Spencer
Cover illustration by Nina Davis
Printed by Hobbs the Printers, Totton

About the Authors

Tim Brown is a Principal Lecturer in Housing Studies at the Centre for Comparative Housing Research at De Montfort University, Leicester. He is joint co-ordinator of the European Network for Housing Research Working Group on Housing Management. He is a corporate member of the Chartered Institute of Housing and is Chairperson of Leicester Newarke Housing Association.

Jon Passmore is Chief Executive of Taff Housing Association having previously been a director at Moat Housing Group and Chief Housing Officer at East Northamptonshire DC. He is a corporate member of the Chartered Institute of Housing. He is a council member of the Chartered Institute of Housing and is an advisory member of the Good Practice Unit.

Dedication
This publication is dedicated to Rosemary and Christopher who have, among other things, had to forego the use of a home computer for a number of weekends; and to Iris for her support, encouragement and advice which enabled this and many other things to come to fruition.

FOREWORD

In the years following the Housing Act 1988, it was clear to housing associations that the name of the game was *Development*. This meant clever tricks with private finance, more homes for less public money, and 'letting Housing Benefit take the strain' as rents rose remorselessly.

In local authorities the position looked very different: the trickle of new council house building petered out, and the key issue was *Housing Management*. But it was easy to be distracted by the agendas of Compulsory Competitive Tendering and local authority cut-backs. There was seldom the resources or the time to think about the wider social issues increasingly impacting upon council estates.

Now, at the end of the 1990s, housing practitioners are becoming familiar with the concept of *Social Exclusion*. And they know it is on the estates which they have developed and managed that a large proportion of those who are excluded from the mainstream society are now living. Many have asked themselves 'is social housing part of the problem, rather than the solution?'.

This Guide seeks to widen horizons, to raise awareness in housing circles of the underlying issues which now impinge directly on all social housing providers. It looks at how housing is central to broader strategies which the government wants to pursue – and vice versa. Past policies of concentrating those on the lowest incomes in particular places – raising rents so that employment is discouraged – can stigmatise and marginalise. But the process also provides opportunities for the owners of those estates, and puts housing practitioners in the front line in the search for solutions.

The Joseph Rowntree Foundation is delighted to be associated with the Chartered Institute of Housing in supporting the preparation and publication of this Guide. Tim Brown and Jon Passmore are to be congratulated on a book which will bring housing practitioners up to speed in a changing world – and help in the recognition that those involved in social housing are central to solving the crushing problems of poverty and exclusion faced by so many.

RICHARD BEST
Director, Joseph Rowntree Foundation
January 1998

ACKNOWLEDGEMENTS

The Chartered Institute of Housing is grateful to Richard Best of the Joseph Rowntree Foundation for his constructive and critical support, and for the considerable financial help given by the Foundation.

The authors would like to thank the Low Pay Unit for access to their library and for providing advice and guidance during the research – in particular Chris Pond MP for his initial support for the publication. Also, thanks to Ross Fraser, Director of Professional Practice, Chartered Institute of Housing, and Tony Trott for their assistance and perseverance.

In addition, the authors would like to thank the following people for their interesting and thought-provoking comments on earlier drafts:

Louise Barnden	Chartered Institute of Housing Wales
Jane Davidson	Welsh Local Government Association
Sarah Elkington	Moat Housing Group
Alan Ferguson	Chartered Institute of Housing Scotland
Mike Frost	Department of the Environment, Transport and the Regions
Marion Keogh	Greater Easterhouse Initiative and Glasgow City Council
John Lambert	Welsh Federation of Housing Associations
Derek Long	Housing Corporation
Rachel Lopata	Leicester City Council
John Perry	Chartered Institute of Housing
Liz Potter	National Housing Federation
Margaret Sandford	People for Action 2001
Richard Spain	National Local Government Forum Against Poverty
Simon Thomas	Wales Council for Voluntary Action
Debby Wheatley	Solihull Metropolitan Borough Council
Jim Whiston	Scottish Homes
Nicola Yates	East Northamptonshire District Council

The authors have also drawn on the knowledge and experiences of a wide and diverse range of practitioners and experts, and greatly appreciate their help and assistance.

Nevertheless in the end the responsibility for the final manuscript is that of the two authors.

About this Guide

'If you are not part of the solution, you are part of the problem'

❑ Purpose of the Guide

During the 1990s, housing organisations both as social landlords, and as strategic enablers, have had to deal increasingly with the symptoms and consequences of poverty. This has resulted in:

- new initiatives in core housing activities in management and development;
- expansion into new areas, such as employment and training; and
- proposals to alter radically the nature of social housing organisations, e.g. Focus Housing Group's initiative to transform the organisation into a social investment agency.

But on the less positive side of the equation:

- housing organisations are often unaware of initiatives taken by other bodies on, for example, community economic development;
- housing initiatives are often ad hoc and fragmented and fail to link in with wider local anti-poverty strategies;
- housing organisations often take a narrow perspective implying that 'poverty is not their concern as their focus is bricks and mortar' (but policies and practices impact on tenants – many of whom are poor);
- housing organisations mistakenly assume that other bodies appreciate that housing is central to anti-poverty initiatives, and that they will be asked to take a major role in such work. The lack of involvement of housing organisations in the early phases of 'welfare to work' in 1997 and 1998 demonstrates this is not the case; and

- housing professionals are failing to engage in discussions on poverty and social exclusion in the way in which the 'movers and shakers in society' are debating these issues. Are we familiar enough, for instance, with the language of 'social capital', 'civic spirit', 'communitarianism' and 'social justice'? These terms may reinforce long-held views about jargon and obscurity. But they are used in crucial policy making forums, and housing organisations must be able to engage in such debates if they want housing provision to be part of tackling poverty and social injustice.

This Good Practice Guide therefore not only aims to highlight interesting initiatives in tackling the symptoms of poverty, but also focuses on:

- the crucially important issues of strategic policy making and partnerships to tackle poverty and social exclusion; and
- improving the ability of housing organisations and professionals to debate the issues in wider forums.

Housing and anti-poverty partnerships and strategies are thus needed which build on, and link with, broader anti-poverty debates and initiatives and ensure that:

- scarce resources are more effectively directed towards poor people;
- services are made more accessible; and
- people have greater control over their own living standards.

More specifically this Good Practice Guide will:

- provide housing staff with a broad understanding of poverty;
- illustrate the effects of poverty and its interaction with bad housing and, for instance, poor health and low educational attainment;
- provide a framework for developing housing and anti-poverty partnerships and strategies which can usefully contribute to more broadly based local anti-poverty policies;
- propose a range of types of initiatives which housing organisations can take as part of a wider policy framework; and
- identify the links between national policy and local strategies and actions.

The text is based on the following propositions:

- housing organisations need to be proactive in tackling poverty;
- they need to tackle it in the way they provide core housing activities as well as through special projects;

- they need to shift away from pragmatic ad hoc responses towards a multi-agency strategic approach which centrally involves local communities;
- they need to locate their policies and actions within the framework of existing local anti-poverty initiatives; and
- there must be a continued commitment to put housing back at the forefront of social welfare policy.

There is nothing new about housing organisations contributing to tackling poverty and social exclusion. The history of the housing movement in this country has many examples of tackling poverty – directly or indirectly. The campaigns for the introduction of council housing in the early part of this century were, in part, inspired by the high cost and poor quality of private rented accommodation. In the 1950s and 1960s, local small-scale housing associations were established in many parts of the UK to provide affordable housing for groups who were excluded from the main housing tenures.

The recent interest in 'housing plus' has publicised a number of impressive initiatives. The case studies in later chapters represent only a small fraction of schemes underway and they are intended as illustrations of what can be done, rather than as models to be copied. In many cases, housing staff have been surprised by the Chartered Institute of Housing's interest in what they see as obvious, but small scale attempts to alleviate the worst effects of poverty. It is exactly these types of initiatives, especially when developed in partnership with local communities, which are more likely, than large flagship projects, to be implemented successfully and reflect local needs. It is important, nevertheless, that small scale schemes fit into a strategic framework for anti-poverty initiatives. Thus this Guide makes no apologies for a primary emphasis on policy and strategy.

❑ Readership

The Guide is aimed, in the first instance at policy makers, strategy planners and service deliverers – including senior managers in housing organisations, housing staff involved in policy and research, and officers interested in identifying possible initiatives to tackle the effects of poverty.

For local authority councillors and registered social landlord board members this book provides an understanding of the poverty debate, as well as a vision for change. Campaigners and members of voluntary agencies concerned about tackling poverty can use the Guide to identify possible action by local housing organisations. Similarly, tenants' and residents' organisations will find examples of innovative actions, and arguments for change. Finally, students on housing and social policy courses interested in the policy and practice aspects of tackling poverty can use this Guide as a textbook.

❑ Structure of the Guide

This Guide is in five parts. The first part (Chapters 1 and 2) analyses the causes and effects of poverty in relation to housing organisations. This is supplemented by Appendices 1 and 2 which provide more details on these important issues. The second part focuses on the local strategic policy making and the partnership dimensions (Chapter 3). The third part describes the types of activities which can form part of a partnership strategy. These focus on housing management, housing development, and wider activities (Chapters 4, 5 and 6). The fourth part draws attention to resource issues, and monitoring and evaluation (Chapter 7). The final part locates local anti-poverty initiatives and strategies within the wider debates about social exclusion and welfare to work.

Readers who are primarily interested in how to develop and implement a housing and anti-poverty strategy, and identifying specific types of projects, may wish to go directly to Chapters 3-7. However, local strategies and specific schemes must be built on a clear understanding of poverty and its relationship to housing organisations. Furthermore, local strategies and initiatives need to be considered within the framework of national economic and welfare policies. These aspects are covered in Chapters 1, 2 and 8, and the Appendices.

At the end of each chapter there is a guide on general reading. There is an appendix for the references in each chapter. There are also appendices on defining and measuring poverty; a glossary of terms; and a list of useful contact organisations drawn from the case studies.

CHAPTER 1

TACKLING POVERTY AND SOCIAL EXCLUSION

❑ Governmental agenda

Tackling poverty and social exclusion is a high profile issue for the Labour Government. This partly reflects increased poverty over recent decades. One in four people were estimated as living on or below the income support level in the early 1990s compared to less than 1 in 7 in 1979.

The growth of poverty and social exclusion over this period has been charted and highlighted by organisations such as the Child Poverty Action Group (CPAG) and Shelter. In the absence of a national government commitment to tackle the issue, 50% of local authorities have developed anti-poverty strategies, or had started doing so, by spring 1997. But charting the changing dimensions of poverty and developing local policies is not enough – a national government commitment is required.

Since May 1997, there has been a series of government initiatives (reflecting earlier Labour Party statements) which together start providing a national framework for tackling poverty, and have considerable relevance for housing organisations. They include:

- the social exclusion unit within the Cabinet Office, announced in August 1997 and formally launched in December that year, and focusing initially on the worst 1,370 council estates;
- the new deal initiative within the welfare to work programme – housing organisations are working as part of local consortia led by the Employment Service to deliver training and job opportunities related to housing for young people;
- the release of local authority capital receipts which involves spending 15% of the resources on welfare to work projects;
- a comprehensive spending review; and
- specific policy and spending reviews, including – housing; urban regeneration; social security; welfare reform and tax and benefits.

All will affect the involvement of housing organisations in anti-poverty work as a result of:

- greater co-ordination of welfare policies at national and local levels – so bringing together, for example, health policies, education and housing strategies; and
- growing emphasis on local housing strategies, co-ordinated with other policy plans, to justify bidding for resources such as the Single Regeneration Budget and Estate Renewal Challenge Fund.

The key message is for housing organisations to work in partnership with other bodies and local communities in strategic policy making, and in delivering anti-poverty programmes. Their business plans, local housing strategies and contributions to other local policy planning systems, such as local economic development strategies, community care plans and local plans, must focus on the role of housing as part of a programme for tackling poverty and social exclusion.

❑ Relevance for housing organisations

Poverty is a complex concept, which is discussed in more detail in the Appendices. There is a growing consensus that about a quarter of the population are living in poverty, with a significant increase in the last two decades. Social housing organisations have been increasingly faced with dealing with the consequences. For example, they are dealing with the complex difficulties associated with so-called problem estates:

The Garths Estate, Sunderland

This estate of 500 flats was opened in 1939 by the North Eastern Housing Association (now Home Housing Association) as part of the Government's regional policy initiatives to provide construction jobs and improve the housing stock. It was modernised in the 1960s, and remodelled in the 1970s. Despite high levels of unemployment, it remained popular and had a strong community identity until the end of the 1980s. However, for complex and inter-linked reasons including the increasing number of young couples and single person households and the murder of a local child, it gained a notorious reputation for high levels of poverty, unemployment, crime and vandalism – an estate which 'housed the underclass and the socially excluded'.

Void levels increased, rent arrears spiralled and lettings became difficult – turnover increased from over 30% to nearly 45% between 1990 and 1991. Home Housing Association is taking radical action. It is replacing 520 flats with 280 new homes and modernising two smaller blocks. Both allocations and estate management are adapted so as to retain and rebuild the community. Home Housing Association is supporting local initiatives, including:

- a self-help community group, which started in 1990 and provides social and educational opportunities as well as crèche facilities; and
- a local co-operative business – the East End Community Shop.

Home Housing Association is also working in partnership with a local training agency and the building contractor to provide training places for local people. By 1996, nearly 40 trainees had been offered employment and the majority of them have gained qualifications.

This example illustrates that innovative approaches are required which go beyond traditional housing management and development. In tackling poverty, social housing organisations must focus on both core and non-core activities. The latter include employment and training initiatives, supporting local community groups, and promoting education projects.

These types of schemes are now generally referred to as housing plus – which is the added value that housing organisations create through their business and service focus, and through their social and community roles. It is essential that such schemes are not developed in an ad hoc manner. Many local organisations are already involved in attempting to tackle poverty, and it is vital that a co-ordinated multi-agency approach is adopted.

But housing organisations have a wider remit than just these activities. Local housing policy, and the research which supports it, also involves addressing the complex issue of poverty in many ways including, for instance, as an indicator of needs.

Resource allocation and indicators of deprivation

The identification of areas of need, including concentrations of poverty is a significant part of housing policy making. For example, the Government and the Housing Corporation in England use the Generalised Needs Index (GNI) and Housing Needs Index (HNI) in the allocation of resources to local authorities and registered social landlords.

The review of the GNI and HNI in the mid 1990s resulted in the use of specific indicators directly associated with poverty, e.g. households receiving support for housing costs. The review confirmed that resource allocation would have regard to multiple deprivation, through the use of a stress area enhancement factor, based on the Department of Environment's Index of Local Conditions. This includes 13 poverty-related indicators such as unemployment, children in low earning households, and income support recipients.

The previous government virtually abandoned measures of need in the allocation of resources in favour of a performance-orientated approach. However, capital resource allocation for local authority housing strategies in England for 1998/99 has been based on 50% needs (through the GNI) and 50% performance. Moreover, the allocation of the Government's capital receipts initiative in England has been two-thirds based on assessed need through the use of the GNI.

These two illustrations highlight five key points.

Firstly, **poverty is a complex and multi-faceted issue** involving a lengthy and confusing array of jargon and statistics – including deprivation, social exclusion and the underclass. These are described in the Appendices.

Secondly, **poverty is affected by the links between global, national and local events**. Changes in international trade, and greater levels of competition can have devastating local effects. But impacts also depend on national welfare strategies, and the social cohesion of communities. For example, housing benefit affects housing poverty through the poverty trap, but benefits advice which maximises take-up can help alleviate the consequences of economic decline. These forces do not necessarily create an underclass exhibiting high levels of multiple-deprivation and social exclusion.

Thirdly, **responses are often reactive rather than proactive**. Housing organisations need to work with others in order to develop proactive strategies to help to prevent the escalating problems of poverty. This requires sophisticated monitoring of key indicators of community well-being. And, it means working with organisations which have already developed anti-poverty strategies, or pioneered innovative projects.

Fourthly, **housing organisations cannot ignore the issues of poverty**. Traditional core activities such as housing management and development may exacerbate the problems, or they can be used to alleviate potential difficulties. They are not neutral in their effects.

And finally, **more radical and innovative approaches can be developed** by housing organisations, by acting strategically and involving other bodies, especially local communities.

❑ Role of housing organisations

These key points would be accepted by many housing organisations. It is, however, crucial to link them both with the day-to-day issues and problems facing housing staff and local people; and with their roles as local housing policy makers and social landlords.

Housing organisations need to examine how poverty affects what they do, and how they respond to it. This starts with a review of their activities and the environment in which they operate – often referred to as a 'social audit'. It is the initial step in the business planning process. It involves identifying stakeholders and their needs, the external environment and an internal organisational analysis of what is provided, how it is provided, and by whom. These processes are described in Chapter 3.

Table 1.1 on page 10 illustrates the issues which need to be examined, both by local authorities as policy makers, and by all social landlords as providers.

Mapping effects and responses in this way shows a housing organisation how far it is already involved in initiatives which impinge on poverty. But the key questions are:

- do these initiatives form a key element of the housing organisation's mission statements?
- are there co-ordinated housing and anti-poverty partnerships and strategies?

Table 1.1: Mapping effects and responses

Local policy making	Social housing landlords
Impact of poverty	
Poverty is not just an issue for social housing. It is also a significant problem facing low income owner occupiers with mortgage arrears. The Bradford & Bingley Building Society are one of the leading mortgage lenders who have developed a mortgage rescue package – see Chapter 2.	Shifting the role of social housing towards welfare housing is not necessarily a problem as long as social housing landlords modify their housing management strategies, e.g. Moat Housing Society have developed a strategy involving a number of initiatives to ensure the maximisation of tenant incomes such as benefits advice, affordable warmth advice, furniture provision and crisis expenditure – see Chapter 3.
Policies for alleviating poverty	
Defining affordability is a crucial task as part of the planning process for new social housing development. This requires an analysis of local incomes to help define targets for the % of affordable housing on land allocated for residential use. Leicester City Council have set a guideline figure of at least 30% on sites of 20 or more units. This was justified in part through a study on housing and affordability – see Chapter 5.	Co-ordinating welfare advice and housing management. East Northamptonshire District Council in assessing housing benefit identify households who are likely to be eligible for family credit. They thus inform both the household and the Government's Family Credit Unit that there may be an entitlement to additional financial support.
Targeting needs	
Housing needs assessments as part of the process of local housing policy making involves identifying geographical areas of need and disadvantaged groups. Indicators of poverty and deprivation are likely to be used – see this Chapter.	In Scotland, four large council housing peripheral estates have been targeted as part of the New Life for Urban Scotland initiative. It involves a multi-agency approach involving Government, local authorities and the local community in tackling, for example, housing management.
Future directions	
Local authorities and other organisations have considerable amounts of geographical data which could be combined to better identify and prioritise areas of poverty and disadvantage. Birmingham City Council is working with other organisations including the Housing Corporation to investigate the potential of geographical information systems (GIS) on this topic.	Studies such as Clapham et al (1996) on citizenship has raised issues about the future direction of housing management, e.g. is the current mix of skills and knowledge of housing staff appropriate for tackling poverty on social housing estates and re-creating communities and building citizenship?

❑ Stakeholders and anti-poverty initiatives

The answers will partly depend on the attitudes of stakeholders – including private and public financial institutions, regulatory bodies, service users and the local community. Local authorities are stakeholders in other social landlords, as well as being strategic planners and landlords in their own right. Each of these stakeholders may have a complex attitude to housing and anti-poverty strategies.

Financial institutions' perspectives are clearly illustrated in the on-going debates over the implementation of local housing companies (see, for example, Wilcox et al, 1993) and similar proposals. They want efficient and effective housing management, and a robust and rigorous financial approach on transferred 'problem' estates. They take a long term perspective, and will only allocate resources where there are persuasive plans to transform the estates into popular neighbourhoods and social cohesive communities. In order to achieve this, local housing companies will need to be committed from the outset to the development and implementation of housing and anti-poverty strategies, as part of community regeneration.

Regulatory and monitoring bodies will be concerned with both value for money, and the wider and longer term accountability to society. Charitable housing associations may be precluded from direct campaigning on anti-poverty initiatives. However government, through its regulators, is concerned with what it gets for taxpayers' money, apart from bricks and mortar. This helps promote a wider stakeholding approach. Performance standards, housing plus, housing quality standards, and now best value, could all include a requirement to adopt an anti-poverty approach.

Service users want improved services but are unlikely to want additional costs. Housing organisations need to avoid making such assumptions. Instead, they must develop a customer research strategy (Passmore and Ferguson, 1994). Tenants on so-called problem estates may be much more concerned about inadequate health care, poor schools and lack of job opportunities than the quality of the housing service (Power and Richardson, 1996).

Finally, there are the views of **local communities** which again may be double-edged. Fear of crime and vandalism, the declining quality of schools, and a deteriorating health service might all contribute to a demand for action to rebuild communities.

More widely, the 12th British Social Attitudes Survey has revealed that parts of the welfare state command relatively little public support – such as additional spending on social housing.

Nevertheless, housing organisations should not regard this with pessimism. The Chief Executive of North British Housing Association, David Cowans, commented at the Chartered Institute of Housing Midlands Branch Conference in 1997 that there is a need to shift attention away from 'housing plus' to 'plus housing'. That is, housing organisations must prove that action on, for example, poor educational attainment or bad health cannot be solved by investment in these areas alone.

It has been estimated that health and other public services are spending £240m per year needlessly because of poor housing (Barrow and Bachan, 1997). The current Government's initiative on health is vital. The Minister for Public Health, Tessa Jowell, acknowledges the links between poor health, poverty, inadequate housing, pollution, and low educational attainment. In July 1997, she stated that:

> *"We want to attack the underlying causes of ill-health and break the cycle of social and economic deprivation and social exclusion."*

The Government plans 'health action zones' to improve people's health by a more integrated approach involving not just health organisations, but also local authorities, the business sector, voluntary bodies and local communities.

❑ Opponents of housing and anti-poverty strategies

Anti-poverty work may make sense and be on the Government's agenda, but there are still obstacles. Taylor-Grooby notes in the 12th British Social Attitudes Survey that:

> *"Public attitudes towards the welfare state are coloured by self-interest rather than altruism. Popular support for 'old welfare' has proved to be robust because it is rooted in the self interest of Britain's contented majority."*

In particular, he found that the contented majority were more strongly in favour of additional spending on universal welfare services such as health, and less committed to spending on residual welfare such as social housing and social security. Attempts to change radically the direction of housing organisations towards an anti-poverty perspective, may not find favour with the contented majority.

During the passage of the Housing Bill in February 1996, the then Government rejected attempts to extend the role of registered social landlords. It argued that it was inappropriate to enable social landlords 'to promote the economic and social well-being of residents'. Yet the advocacy of a housing and anti-poverty strategy is primarily geared to housing organisations contributing to community regeneration.

There are, thus, external factors to be overcome. There are also factors internal to housing organisations and the housing profession which could limit these activities. The traditional view of the core activities of housing development and management often results in reluctance to get involved in housing and anti-poverty initiatives. Some practitioners consider that tackling poverty and social exclusion is not relevant to, nor part of, the remit of housing organisations. But housing management and development are not neutral activities. They can contribute, directly or indirectly, to making poverty worse.

At the opposite end of the spectrum, some practitioners, who acknowledge the contribution which housing may make to increasing poverty and hardship, consider that the potential for action is too limited to make the effort worthwhile. Others avoid acting because the fundamental causes are outside their immediate control. Both these views fail to recognise that anti-poverty initiatives can reduce the impact of macro-economic policy and broader environmental changes.

❑ Overcoming scepticism

The adoption of housing and anti-poverty initiatives is not without problems. Some stakeholders may be reluctant to support such approaches, while external factors may also limit their effectiveness. Moreover, housing professionals have differing views over the relevance of such initiatives.

However, many of the routine difficulties and problems faced by local housing policy makers and social housing landlords stem from the effects of poverty and social exclusion. Housing organisations need to become involved in anti-poverty initiatives in order to be more effective. They have the opportunity to work with the many potential allies who outweigh the sceptics. These include:

- other local government departments, e.g. economic development units, community development departments and low pay units;

- professional bodies such as the British Medical Association;
- organisations representing poverty campaigns such as the Low Pay Unit, the Child Poverty Action Group, and Shelter; and
- local communities campaigning against poverty and social exclusion.

Guide to further reading

Government policy on poverty and social exclusion
There is no single up-to-date guide on this primarily because policy is changing so quickly. Readers are advised to view weekly, monthly and bi-monthly journals and magazines such as *Agenda, Housing, Housing Today, Inside Housing, New Statesman, Labour Research,* and *Roof.*

Relationship between housing and social policy
The links between housing and other aspects of welfare are explored in Chartered Institute of Housing (1995): *A Point to Prove*: Coventry, CIH. A more general coverage of the relationship between health, poverty, and unemployment can be found in Wilkinson R (1996): *Unhealthy Societies*: London, Routledge.

Stakeholding and citizenship
The role of housing in promoting citizenship is discussed in some detail in Clapham D et al (1996): *Citizenship and Housing – Shaping the Debate*: Coventry, CIH.
More general coverage of the debates on citizenship and a stakeholder society can be found in Hutton's work, particularly Hutton W (1995): *The State We're In*: London, Jonathan Cape and in an interview in the May 1997 edition of *Housing* between Will Hatchett and Will Hutton.

CHAPTER 2

POVERTY AND HOUSING

This chapter identifies the way poverty issues affect the various housing sectors, and the impact on the work of housing organisations. It considers:

- social rented sector;
- owner occupation;
- private rented sector; and
- homelessness.

❑ Social rented sector

■ Incomes

Council housing has become housing for the poor. The average gross weekly income for heads of households in council housing in England for 1995/6 was £144 compared to £340 for all tenures (Green et al, 1997). New tenants are the least well off in society. Residualisation – the process by which poor housing, poor households and low political profile are combined – has become a major force in shaping the housing system (Malpass and Murie, 1994). The affluent skilled and employed working class households have gradually switched tenure to become owner occupiers, while the economically inactive and unemployed have become council tenants. This is part of a larger restructuring of the housing market, encouraged by governments since the 1950s. They have promoted owner occupation as the tenure of choice, using public subsidy to increase its attractiveness. The effect has been a growing concentration in local authority housing of those unable to buy.

There are similar trends in housing associations, particularly in new lettings, prompting some to take action. They have begun to consider the types of homes they are providing, who they are housing and how they can sustain the new tenancies which they are creating.

In the mid 1980s, associations were generally housing low income but economically active households. By the mid 1990s new association tenants were increasingly unemployed. These changes are supported by statistical data on average gross weekly incomes. Incomes for housing association tenants in 1995/96 averaged £179, a figure significantly below the national average of £381.

Research on social housing in England summarises the current situation:

> *"The demographic profile of the population housed in the social rented sector has been fundamentally altered ... the age distribution of heads of households is now bimodal with ... humps being centred around those in the mid 70s and those ... in their mid 20s. Households ... with economically active heads are significantly more likely to leave the sector."* (Burrows, 1997)

■ Affordability

The affordability of rents now dominates the housing debate. It is aggravated by recent sharp rent rises and falling incomes of the poorest in society. As with poverty, there is uncertainty over the definition of affordability. And, definitions have changed in response to changing factors, particularly the impact of private finance on housing association rents.

The National Housing Federation used three definitions, in as many years, in the early 1990s:

- 1990: Rents should account for no more than 20% of average household incomes;
- 1991: Rents should not breach 22% of average household incomes based on the ratio between gross rents and net income; and
- 1993: Rents are affordable if the majority of working households taking up new tenancies are not caught in the poverty trap (because of dependency on housing benefit) or paying more than 25% of net income on rent.

Historically, there has been a high degree of consistency between local authority rents and average gross male incomes from the 1950s to the 1980s (Wilcox, 1994). In the mid 1950s local authority rents averaged 6.7% of average earnings. This fluctuated during the 1960s and 1970s between

7%-8.5%. By the 1980s rents were rising in the local authority sector, and maintained a range of 9%-10%. In the 1990s this changed as the new financial regime introduced by the Housing and Local Government Act 1989 fed through. By 1994 local authority rents in England had risen to 12.7% of gross average income.

Housing association sector rents were always marginally higher because of differences in the subsidy regime. They also reflected a slighter higher income group, often newer accommodation and higher management costs of more dispersed stock. During the 1980s rents fluctuated around 12% of average gross incomes. With the increased reliance on private finance following the Housing Act 1988 this rose in the early 1990s to 14%, on assured lettings. By 1994 it had risen to 16.2% in England, with fair rents only marginally behind at 14.6%.

The position in Wales and Scotland for housing association assured lettings offers an interesting comparison. In Wales rent increases have followed a similar path, rising to 15.8% of earnings by 1994. In Scotland the rise has been less sharp and the overall trend less clear. By 1994 assured rents remained at 10.3% of earnings.

While rents have been rising rapidly in the association and council sectors, incomes from those occupying social housing have been falling. While average real incomes between 1979 and 1992 have risen by 37% after housing costs, for those in the bottom 10% of the income league, real incomes after housing costs had fallen by 18% (Department of Social Security, 1993).

■ Rent setting

In relation to affordability policies for the housing association sector, until the 1995 bid round, rents did not influence allocations by the Housing Corporation. They were forced up as capital grants were reduced. The bidding regime adopted by the Housing Corporation in 1997/8, tried to re-focus attention on affordability by limiting rent increases.

The approach in Wales has been substantially different, with Tai Cymru balancing rents and capital costs. The arrangements adopted for 1997/8 funding were based on benchmark rents for seven property types. Registered social landlords were invited to reduce rents on all properties to the benchmarks to qualify for Social Housing Grant. Concern has been expressed that the benchmark rents and the future increase model of RPI minus 1% are too low. Further, the policy takes no account of the financial position of individual housing associations. The short term effect of the policy has been to significantly reduce surpluses. In the medium term, it will force the majority of housing associations into deficit. Its overall success in reducing rents however may make it an attractive model beyond Wales.

In Scotland, average housing association rents are similar to local authority rents. By implication, this is a result of policy, and shows a greater commitment to bricks and mortar subsidy than south of the Border. However there are significant local variations – an example later in this chapter shows that housing association rents in Easterhouse in Glasgow are up to £8 a week lower than equivalent council rents.

In Scotland and Wales, devolution could cause new tensions in rent setting. The Scottish Parliament, for example, will be responsible for housing policy including rents, but the UK Parliament will have a major say on the social security budget including housing benefit.

■ The unemployment and poverty trap

The welfare system keeps large numbers on benefits because of inadequate incentives, such as tapers and in-work benefits, to get people back to work. We now have the consequences of the previous policy that housing association rents should be raised, and housing benefit would take the strain. This is often referred to as a benefits trap. In reality, it is also a tax and poverty trap, as an individual has only to earn £80 a week before having to pay tax at 20%. This poverty trap is particularly important in relation to rent setting. Thus, as the later case studies indicate, benefits advice as well as rent-setting faces an uphill struggle without radical reforms to the benefit system. The welfare system locks people into benefit and unemployment through the withdrawal of benefit at a rapid rate. So when travel to work costs, lunch and child care costs are included, it is economically preferable to remain at home. Table 2.1 shows how little is left from an extra pound of earnings.

Table 2.1 demonstrates the dramatic effect of tax and benefit withdrawal – as rents rise, the depth and length of the trap grows.

At £50 weekly rent, a family will need to earn £250 to escape tax and benefit withdrawal. At £70 per week, the same family's income needs to rise above £290 for them to get any significant financial benefit.

This does not just affect the household. Economic inactivity increases costs to the Exchequer. It also impacts at the local level on arrears, household budgeting and arguably on crime and the informal economy. It has even been suggested that the ultimate test of affordability is the extent households get into arrears.

Table 2.1: Benefits trap – deductions from £1 gross earnings

	Family		Single/couple	
Tax/Benefit	deduction	balance	Deduction	balance
Income tax	20p		20p	
National insurance	10p		10p	
Net Earnings		70p		70p
Family credit @ 70%	49p			
Income net of Family Credit		21p		
Housing Benefit @ 65%	14p		45.5p	
Council tax @ 20%	4p		14p	
Net disposable income		3p		10.5p

Based on rates for 1997/98

■ Arrears

The lowest income groups do not experience the highest arrears, due to the protection of the benefits system. Instead, those who are in lowest paid employment, or go on and off benefits, are most likely to experience arrears. The risk increases with the number of dependants, or where there is a change in family circumstances such as employment loss, birth of a child, or death (Kempson, 1993). Thus those at the greatest risk are working lone parents and families with three or more children.

In relation to future affordability levels, there is little sign yet that government policy will bring rents down, even if rates of increase are slowed. This reinforces the importance of social landlords taking a proactive approach to housing and anti-poverty work.

■ Affordability policies

In England, a number of housing associations operate affordability policies.

The **William Sutton Trust** has had an affordability policy since 1994. Initial use of NHF indicator rents did not adequately reflect local situations. The policy is based on the following guidelines which take account of local preferences and demand:

- matrix of rent points which reflect size, amenity and location;
- equalising rents on assured and secure tenancies;
- setting a maximum annual rent increase; and
- setting a maximum rent for each property size by region.

The **Guinness Trust** manages 13,000 tenancies, predominantly in the South and Midlands. It has a substantial property base developed partly from charitable sources, and has substantial reserves. The Trust sets an income bar on applicants, in order to meet its charitable objectives.

It commissioned Steve Wilcox to examine its rent setting, affordability and the income bar – particularly in the light of the wide regional differentials in house prices compared with narrow differentials in incomes. In some parts of the country an individual, who would be eligible for housing benefit in rented housing, can afford to buy at the lower end of the market.

The research offered three routes forward to establish an affordable rents policy:

- NHF affordability matrix; or
- 25% of net income for working households; or
- a comparative matrix.

The application of the NHF model would have increased the proportion of single and childless couples who would become benefit dependent, as rents would rise for these groups.

The second model was the Trust's existing policy that households should not pay more than 25% of their net income on their rent. However, it did not take account of service charges, and impacted unevenly on elderly households who lost out as a result of benefit loss due to capital savings. It also took no account of the residual income needed by larger households.

The third option was a comparative policy based on four premises:

- households with incomes at the level of the Trust's income bar should not need to rely on housing benefit to pay a Trust rent;
- households with incomes at the level of average earnings should not need to rely on housing benefit to pay a Trust rent;
- Trust rents should not be greater than average private rents for properties of the same size; and
- rents should stand in a coherent pattern related to property size.

This gives rents a combined housing market and income base. Taking a couple with two children in a three bedroom dwelling as the central point, the average earnings and income bar matrices were adjusted to achieve a coherent pattern. A review of private sector rents was then used to calculate rents for other dwelling sizes, based on a percentage variation. The final outcome is a rents policy which varies by region and property type. It combines issues of affordability based on income levels, as well as lettability, by ensuring Trust rents are competitive with private rents in any region.

Guinness adopted the third option. One subsequent lesson they learnt is that it is extremely difficult to relate rents to local variations in the micro-economic climates.

❑ Owner occupation

Nearly 70% of households are in the owner occupied sector. It is a diverse tenure that includes nearly 30% of households with the lowest 10% of gross income. Over 40% of owner occupiers own their property outright in England. Many of them are asset rich but revenue poor. They have low fixed incomes which are barely adequate to meet day-to-day living costs including housing repairs, but they have a valuable asset – their home. However, nearly 60% of owner occupiers have a mortgage and about 15% of them have difficulty meeting their payments, and risk repossession. Housing and anti-poverty strategies, thus need to cover owner occupation as well as the social rented sector. This includes advice and guidance to potential home owners on the risks.

The growth and changing characteristics of the owner occupied sector are complex, but the key features relevant to poverty, from a recent study by Green et al (1997) are:

- there are an increasing number of elderly owner occupiers. They have risen from 50% in 1984 to over 60% a decade later. This trend will continue because the population group below them (aged 45 to 64) increased from 63% to 77% in the same period; and
- people in the lowest income groups spend up to 80% of their gross income on mortgage payments.

■ Repossessions

The scale of negative equity is declining from a peak of 1.8m households in early 1992 (Wilcox, 1996). But it remains an issue for about 1m households, and mortgage arrears and repossessions are still at the high levels of the late 1980s. The latter are still running on average at over 800 per week, while nearly 0.4m households are three months or more in arrears with their mortgage payments. Nearly 15% of mortgagors have difficulties with their payments (Green et al, 1997). Households in arrears are most likely to be those where the head of household is unemployed, or where the gross weekly income is less than £100 per week, or where the household is a lone parent family.

■ Conditions

The 1991 English House Condition Survey estimated that 5.5% of owner occupied dwellings were unfit. In Scotland, nearly 4% of owner occupied dwellings are below tolerable standards, while in Wales, 12% of the owner occupied stock is unfit. It has been estimated that there are over 0.9m owner occupied properties in the UK which were either unfit or, in the case of Scotland, below the tolerable standard, while a further 2.5m owner occupied dwellings were in need of urgent repairs of at least £1,000 (Leather and Morrison, 1997). The poor condition of owner-occupied housing particularly impacts on certain groups. Nearly 80% of South Asian households are owner occupiers; over a third of them live in over-crowded conditions; and this pattern of poor quality owner occupied housing has been remarkably persistent over time (Brown and Passmore, 1996).

■ Vulnerable groups

Home ownership remains beyond the reach of most people on low incomes, and 'owner occupation can become a route into long term poverty' (Kempson, 1996). She identifies particular problems for:

- minority ethnic households;
- elderly households;

- young people;
- households in rural areas; and
- those on low incomes and insecure employment.

Owner occupation may not be in the best interests of low income households, yet housing aspirations together with constraints in the social rented sector make an increase in problematic home ownership likely. Housing and anti-poverty strategies must not only identify and react to existing problems, but also be proactive in promoting more sustainable home ownership initiatives. There are three areas in which specific action can be taken:

- home ownership and debts;
- disrepair; and
- low cost home ownership, including shared ownership.

The Chartered Institute of Housing has published a study on sustainable home ownership (CIH, 1997). This highlights, among other things, the steps which are needed to avoid the problems faced by potential low income owner occupiers. They include five goals for sustainable home ownership policy:

- it must contribute to sustainable economic prosperity by avoiding volatility in housing markets through, for example, counter cyclical changes (such as the abolition of MIRAS) when housing prices are rising;
- it must be sustainable for those who become owner occupiers and there must be adequate alternatives for those who do not take up owner occupation;
- it must encourage the maintenance and repair of owner occupied properties, e.g. the use of property logbooks;
- it must contribute to environmental sustainability, e.g. minimum energy efficiency standards; and
- it must be sustainable in public subsidy terms.

■ Home ownership and debts

Households which are having difficulties with mortgage payments may also have other debts. For example, over 10% of households with a net weekly income of less than £100 have three or more outstanding debts (Berthoud and Kempson, 1992). Money management and budgeting styles therefore become crucial aspects of a coping strategy. Households who adopt a planned budget approach are less likely to fall further behind with their bills – including mortgage repayments (Kempson, 1996).

Housing and anti-poverty strategies need to cover debts facing owner occupiers. The 1991 mortgage rescue package by building societies and housing associations failed to appreciate the breadth and complexity of multiple debt. Nevertheless, a few mortgage lenders have developed innovative practices with housing associations and local authorities.

The **Bradford & Bingley Building Society** had, by 1996, contributed £60 million to schemes to allow 1,200 borrowers in financial difficulty to remain in their homes. It works with two housing association partners – English Churches Housing Group and Circle 33 Housing Trust – who, with the Building Society, have set up par value mutual housing associations, to purchase and own the houses. The Society's mortgage rescue unit provides advice and guidance to applicants wishing to join the scheme. Applicants must be in serious mortgage arrears, in negative equity and be entitled to 100% housing benefit.

In addition, the Building Society has:

- produced a debt action pack for staff and customers;
- established a mortgage rescue unit; and
- provided advice on welfare benefits to its customers.

Liaison and partnerships with mortgage lenders on both an individual and a policy basis is therefore a necessary but not sufficient approach. An integrated approach is also required which co-ordinates the diverse range of support services which homeowners may turn to when debt becomes a severe problem.

In **Leicester**, for instance, there are a wide range of agencies which may offer advice including:

- Benefits Agency offices;
- Law centres such as the Highfields and Belgrave Law Centre;
- Leicester Citizens' Advice Bureau;
- Leicester City Council's Housing Advice Centre;
- Leicester City Council's Money Advice Unit;

- Leicestershire County Council's Social Services Welfare Rights Team;
- Mortgage Lenders such as building societies; and
- Shelter's Housing Advice Project.

Each of these agencies could unintentionally take a narrow perspective of a home owner's debts problems. However Leicester City Council's Anti-Poverty Collection and Debt Recovery Strategy establishes a co-ordinated corporate approach for dealing with debt. Mortgage arrears are, of course, primarily dealt with by mortgage lenders, but households with multiple debts could have financial problems associated with the payment of Council Tax as well as failing to claim all available welfare benefits. A wider partnership approach on aspects such as debt recovery and money advice is thus clearly required so as to extend this type of activity and provide a one-stop shop for owner occupiers with debt problems.

Disrepair

Low income home owners do not have the financial resources to maintain their dwellings. Changes in the availability of grants for repair and improvement, both in terms of total budgets, and in terms of discretionary systems (under the Housing, Construction and Regeneration Act 1996) mean that very few will get external subsidy to deal with disrepair. Similar effects are being felt in Scotland following the removal of the 'ring fence' on private sector renewal funds.

Nevertheless, many initiatives have been pioneered by local authorities, housing associations and voluntary sector organisations to tackle these problems including:

- home improvement agencies, care and repair projects/staying put schemes; and
- area caretakers/urban management officers who have advisory, educational and promotional roles in helping home owners maintain their properties.

The Joseph Rowntree Foundation is now funding a major research project on the maintenance and upkeep of owner occupied property, including studies on the attitudes of owners and the lessons which can be learnt from other Western European countries.

Care and repair schemes are run by independent agencies, funded by central and local government, to assist vulnerable people to make use of the grant system and other sources of finance for improvement, repair and adaptation. These agencies liaise with local government departments such as housing and social services as well as with voluntary sector bodies. They also help to organise the selection of a builder as well as supervising the work. In 1996, 200 care and repair agencies in England carried out work worth £45 million which benefited approximately 27,000 vulnerable people.

Lack of resources to fund such initiatives remains a fundamental difficulty. Private owners need to invest more on property maintenance. Those on low incomes may be unable to repay any further borrowing against the value of their home.

They could participate in equity share loans – whereby they assign a share of the market value of a property to a lender in lieu of repayments. But the scale of activity in this area is extremely small. Studies on the use of equity-release mechanisms suggest that, although it is most commonly used by elderly households, it is principally used to fund everyday living costs especially household bills (Davey, 1997). Only about 25% of households used the funds for house repair and improvements and much of that figure was spent on redecoration.

Housing and anti-poverty strategies need to include low income home owners living in poorly maintained properties. Local authority housing improvement strategies need to incorporate good practice and advice for existing and potential owners about maintenance issues, as well as providing help and support in respect of welfare benefit eligibility.

■ Low cost home ownership including shared ownership

Since the 1970s, low cost home ownership has been promoted in various forms. The previous Government encouraged many households to get a foot on the ownership ladder in the 1990s through such initiatives. Research in the early 1990s had suggested that shared ownership could, in certain localities, be an extremely important mechanism for providing affordable housing (Bramley, 1991).

Low cost home ownership initiatives have included:

- discounted purchase (notably in conjunction with the right to buy);

- shared ownership;
- Tenants' Incentive Scheme;
- Tai Cymru's Homebuy Option Scheme;
- self-build;
- Joseph Rowntree Foundation's Flexible Tenure; and
- equity loan schemes.

However since the mid 1990s, the Housing Corporation, Scottish Homes and Tai Cymru have been curtailing some of these initiatives.

Low cost home ownership schemes and especially shared ownership schemes are likely to be most relevant in areas where house prices are relatively high – where there is a significant gap between social renting and the bottom rungs of the owner occupied ladder. In areas, such as parts of the East Midlands, however, where house prices are significantly below the national average, there will be only a narrow band of households for whom shared ownership (or other alternatives) would be financially more attractive than social renting or full owner occupation.

A major issue in respect of shared ownership is its limited flexibility. It assumes rising incomes, but those in employment may only have part time work, or short term contracts. Should a person working in an uncertain labour market take on the obligations of shared ownership? It would be more effective if it allowed a smaller starting share, and the ability to decrease the ownership stake in times of financial difficulties, as well as increase it in times of relative affluence.

Low cost ownership schemes have other benefits, even where they are not cheaper than renting, such as reducing demand for social rented property, and contributing to more varied communities on social housing estates. But the benefit for low income households may in some cases be marginal. Housing organisations need therefore to carry out detailed investigations on the appropriateness of low cost home ownership to meet the needs of specific groups, such as minority ethnic households, and avoid creating additional poverty by enticing households to enter owner occupation unwisely.

❑ Private renting

The private rented sector is a diverse and fragmented tenure – being much more heterogeneous than the social rented sector. Poverty and poor quality accommodation are common factors for some groups living in this sector. A Department of the Environment study of the sector found that:

- the proportion of tenants who are unemployed had increased from 5% in 1990 to 14% in 1993/94;
- the proportion of tenants under 30 years of age, who tend to have lower incomes, had increased from 29% in 1988 to nearly 40% in 1993/94; and
- nearly 15% of tenancies were sharing (or lacking) a kitchen or at least one basic amenity (Carey, 1995).

The sector, however, continues to be dominated by individual landlords (Wilcox, 1994). There has been a rapid decline of regulated tenancies and an increase in assured shorthold tenancies. Nearly 15% of households with the lowest 10% of gross incomes were in the private rented sector in 1994/95. In relation to household types, one person households (especially elderly households) are over-represented in the unfurnished sector, while young single persons and multi-person non-family households are more likely to be found in the furnished sector.

Although the sector is important in meeting housing needs, Wilcox (1996) has pointed out that 'it would be rash to anticipate any continuing growth in the years ahead' because of the modest recovery in the owner occupied market as well as recent housing benefit changes. The use of the private rented sector to meet diverse housing needs requires a generous housing benefit system. That cuts across the policy objectives of the Department of Social Security to target expenditure more effectively (Holmans, 1996). Restrictions on housing benefit make it more difficult for some households, such as those with special needs and young people under 25, to use the private rented sector. People reliant on income support also have difficulty meeting any shortfall between the rent and housing benefit.

Local authorities, in conjunction with housing associations and other agencies, have initiated a range of practices which attempt to both enhance the sustainability of the sector and support low income private tenants. The Chartered Institute of Housing (1995) produced a Good Practice Briefing which provides a comprehensive focus on possible action. This includes:

- **rent and deposit guarantee schemes** which help to secure tenancies for low income households and are now operated by many local authorities;

- commitment to a **specified level of service on housing benefits** for tenants of private landlords – as developed by many local authorities including the London Boroughs of Brent and Camden. The London Borough of Ealing, for instance, has fast tracked housing benefit claims of non-priority single homeless people in bed and breakfast accommodation; and
- **local accreditation schemes** including registration for landlords who meet specified standards of accommodation – as developed, for example, by Derby City Council.

A guarantee scheme was introduced by **Colchester Borough Council** in December 1992. The rent deposit element covers the loss or damage to the property of up to £100 for the first 6 months of the assured tenancy. The rent guarantee element ensures that the landlord receives the first three weeks rent within 7 weeks of the start of the tenancy, whether or not a tenant's housing benefit claim is successful. All properties within the scheme are inspected by environmental health officers.

SmartMove

Crisis, a voluntary organisation working for homeless people, set up this franchise scheme in 1997 to support tenants in getting accommodation. Crisis does not run the service itself, but provides training and support including relevant documentation for organisations wishing to establish the project in a particular locality. The services offered through SmartMove include:

- vetting landlords and their properties;
- offering landlords rent in advance and a financial guarantee against loss or damage;
- offering landlords support and advice including assistance when drafting tenancy agreements;
- operating a resettlement service to support new tenants;
- encouraging tenants to save towards their next deposit; and
- acting as a mediator between landlords and tenants.

Tighter regulations governing the availability of housing benefits, however, deter landlords from providing accommodation for low income households, specifically:

- the single room rate restriction for applicants under 25 years old; and
- the capping of rent levels eligible for housing benefit.

❑ Homelessness

As with poverty and affordability, the definition and collection of information on homelessness is fraught with difficulties. Nevertheless, the scale of homelessness is clearly evident from the following statistics:

- homelessness acceptances by local authorities in Great Britain rose from 63,000 households in 1978 to a peak of 173,000 in 1992. It has now fallen to around 150,000 per year;
- homeless applications have also risen significantly. In the case of Scotland, the number of households applying as homeless rose from 15,500 in 1983/84 to 43,000 in 1993/94: and
- the number of homeless households in temporary accommodation in England rose from just over 4,000 in 1980 to a peak of 63,000 in 1992. It is now running at about 45,000 per year.

Homelessness is linked with poverty – for example, over 10% of homeless applicant households gave mortgage arrears and rent arrears as the main cause. This is likely to be an underestimate, as records only give a single reason for homelessness. Most research shows that the reasons for homelessness are complex and multi-dimensional (Oppenheim and Harker, 1996).

Restrictions on the availability of housing benefit described in the previous section, are likely to have exacerbated the situation.

There are important limitations on the official data on homelessness. Government statistics on incomes such as 'households below average incomes' do not include people living in temporary accommodation or sleeping rough. In addition, there is no comprehensive information on the number of rough sleepers. In Scotland, the 1991 census recorded that there were only 145 people living on the streets of Scotland, yet it is generally recognised that this was a vast underestimate. Shelter (Scotland) considers that the figure may be over 1,000 (Yanetta and Edwards, 1996).

Homelessness and poor housing also affects the education of children (Power et al, 1995). Educational progress is hindered by frequent school changes and poor attendance. Nearly 90% of head teachers consider that homelessness impaired academic performance.

In relation to young people (10-18 year olds) and homelessness, research reveals that:

- 180,000 British children experience homelessness each year;
- in 1990, it was estimated that 43,000 young people ran away from home over 100,000 times; and
- over 40% of homelessness among 16-17 year olds is the direct result of leaving care (Dennehy et al, 1997).

Initiatives tackling homelessness and poverty include:

- hostel provision;
- women's refuges;
- foyers;
- private sector leasing;
- social housing over shops (SHOS);
- housing associations as managing agents (HAMA and HAMA Plus); and
- the rough sleepers' initiative.

In some cases, however, although rooflessness is tackled, the temporary nature of the accommodation which is provided fails to resolve other issues such as children's education (Power et al, 1995).

Foyers tackle the no job/no home cycle affecting young people. They are being developed in both urban and rural areas. The concept comes from France where there are between 450-500 Foyers. In Britain, there are now over 50 projects either in operation or being developed. There are indications that the Labour Government is keen to progress this initiative. The Foyers provide accommodation for young single people (16-24 year olds) as well as offering vocational training for up to two years and welfare counselling services.

Sleaford Foyer, Leicester Housing Association

This was the first purpose-built Foyer in the UK and was opened in 1994 in Sleaford in Lincolnshire. It consists of a 14 bedspace shared house together with 8 x 2 bed houses and 12 x 1 bed flats as well as a training complex and offices/meeting rooms. Capital funding came from a number of sources including North Kesteven District Council (through DoE Partnership Funds), private finance, Leicester Housing Association reserves and development funding through housing association grant.

Between 1994 and 1997, nearly 200 young people have been provided with accommodation and help with training and employment. The major sources of referral have been by word of mouth (45%) and through social services (over 20%). Two-thirds of young people originally lived within three miles of the project.

In terms of outputs, between 1994 and 1997:

- 117 residents were involved in job search at the start of their tenancy, but this had fallen to 55 at the end of their tenancy;
- 11 residents were in employment at the start of their tenancy but this increased to 46 at the end of their tenancy;
- 31 residents were in training at the start of their tenancy compared to 42 at the end of their tenancy; and
- 21 residents were attending a college course at the start of their tenancy compared to 29 at the end of their tenancy.

❑ Summary

This chapter illustrates the role of housing organisations in confronting poverty in the public, private and voluntary sectors. However, there are difficulties and concerns with these approaches:

- innovative approaches (e.g. Care and Repair schemes and Foyer projects) attempt to resolve poverty-related issues in a non-standard manner. However, they may divert attention away from core activities such as housing management and housing development;

- core activities (e.g. rent affordability models) and non-core innovative approaches are being developed by many housing organisations, but not necessarily in an integrated way;
- initiatives taken by housing organisations are often **not** part of a co-ordinated multi-agency partnership and strategy for tackling poverty and social exclusion; and
- there has been little internal monitoring and evaluation of effectiveness.

These points are illustrated in the following two examples relating to social housing rents:

Bradford City Challenge supported the development of 400 new housing association properties on the Homewood Estate – the out-turn rents were on average over £60 per week compared to the local authority rents for the other 3,400 properties of £36 per week on average. The former Chief Executive of Bradford City Challenge, speaking at the Chartered Institute of Housing Annual Conference in 1997, commented that the new development created benefit dependency and made it more difficult to create a sustainable community.

Greater Easterhouse comprises a series of large local authority estates on the edge of Glasgow housing over 40,000 people. There is a high level of poverty with 80% of households having no car and nearly 70% of children being entitled to free school meals. Since the 1980s, eight housing associations and co-operatives have been active in redevelopment work. There are, however, a number of major rent anomalies including:

- council rents for four bedroom flats are £6-£8 per week higher than for housing associations and co-operatives; and
- housing association and co-operative rents, nevertheless, tend to be higher on peripheral estates than in the inner areas where there are more facilities.

Again, this suggests a lack of co-ordination leading to potential difficulties in alleviating poverty and social exclusion.

These issues are more broadly illustrated in the following example drawn from a large city in England.

The local authority is developing a corporate anti-poverty strategy, but so far the housing department has not been directly involved. Nevertheless, there have been housing-related initiatives, such as welfare benefit take-up campaigns on specific estates and the development of affordable warmth campaigns as part of an energy efficiency strategy. Considerable attention has been paid to low income homeowners in terms of disrepair. There is a care and repair home improvement agency in operation. There has also been considerable work undertaken on housing and affordability.

There are 20 housing associations operating in the area and a number of them have also focused attention on aspects of anti-poverty work such as affordable warmth. Currently there is an on-going debate about the potential for establishing a foyer scheme.

However there are large variations in housing associations rents for similar property in the same locality.

	Average Rents (£ a week in 1995) per Housing Association	
	1 Bedroom Property	**3 Bedroom Property**
Highest	£44.43	£60.24
Mean	£34.56	£43.86
Lowest	£29.07	£31.83

Housing association tenants may therefore have to contend with major affordability and poverty problems depending on which housing association is their landlord.

Thus, in this case study, there is evidence to suggest a need for individual housing associations to consider whether their rent levels undermine their general housing objectives.

The role of housing organisations in tackling the causes of poverty is limited, but they are faced with dealing with the symptoms of the problem. Currently there are a number of innovative approaches as well as some interest in rethinking the relevance of core activities. The key issue, which is the focus of the next chapter, is thus the development of a strategic approach.

Guide to further reading

Dealing with poverty

The following texts provide an overview of the role of housing organisations in dealing with the symptoms of poverty:

Brown T and Passmore J (1996): *Poverty and Social Housing*: Sevenoaks, Moat Housing Group

Power A with Richardson L (1996): *Housing Plus – An Agenda for Social Landlords?*: London, London School of Economics

In relation to specific types of initiatives, the following are recommended:

Foyers

Foyer Federation for Youth (1997): *Foyer Handbook – A Guide for Developers and Managers of Foyers*: London, FFY

Foyer Federation for Youth (1997): *Opening Doors for Young People*: London, FFY

Mortgage rescue schemes

Bradford & Bingley Building Society (1994): *Mortgage Rescue – Making it Work*

Private rented sector

Chartered Institute of Housing (1995): *Meeting Housing Needs in the Private Rented Sector*: Coventry, CIH Good Practice Briefing No 1

Bayley R (1997): Housing Innovations in the Firing Line: *Roof*, May/June

Chapter 3

Acting Strategically

This chapter:

- offers guidance on how to develop a housing and anti-poverty strategy; and
- identifies the organisational and inter-organisational frameworks needed to make it part of a broader local strategy to tackle social exclusion.

Social housing has increasingly become residualised, while both owner occupation and private renting have significant problems associated with poverty. Some social housing organisations have developed innovative practices to reduce the impact of poverty and social exclusion. This is a necessary response, but is it sufficient?

❑ The need for co-ordination

Housing organisations need comprehensive and co-ordinated approaches for tackling poverty and social exclusion, through a strategic or policy-orientated framework. However, they are not the only interested agencies, and need to work with others on both policy formulation and implementation (see Chapter 1). Strategies need to be co-ordinated within the framework of other local policy planning systems, such as:

- housing investment programmes;
- local housing strategies;
- community care plans;
- existing local anti-poverty strategies; and
- local economic development strategies.

In the housing field, examples of local authorities and housing associations working together abound and have been well illustrated by Fraser (1990). In 1997, the Chartered Institute of Housing, the Local Government Association and the National Housing Federation produced a pamphlet on *Making Partnerships Work*. But policy co-ordination within and between organisations is not an automatic and unproblematic area.

Delivering 'Welfare to Work' and the 'New Deal'

(see also Chapter 8)
An important theme of Government policy to tackle poverty and social exclusion has been the 'welfare to work' initiatives launched in 1997. These included two specific schemes relevant to housing organisations:

- the release of capital receipts requirement that at least 15% of resources be channelled into 'welfare to work' projects; and
- the 'new deal' for 18-24 year olds who had been on job seeker's allowance for more than 6 months.

In both cases, the response of housing organisations by the end of 1997 had been far from satisfactory. In relation to the former, the tight deadlines for detailed overall submissions on the use of the release of capital receipts prevented liaison with other organisations especially local consortia concerned with the delivery of the 'new deal'. In relation to the latter, housing organisations were rarely members of these consortia, led by the Employment Service and involving bodies such as local TECs and other education and training institutions.

Housing organisations appeared to assume that these bodies appreciated the relevance of housing and were waiting to be asked to participate. Moreover, the Government and these other bodies anticipated that housing organisations would have explicit strategies which identified the nature of the relationship between housing and poverty as well as having a costed set of proposals.

Housing organisations need to learn the following lessons from these experiences if they are to participate in the next stages of the 'new deal' in late 1998 and 1999:

- factors such as tight deadlines make partnership building difficult, but this must be taken account of in the planning process;

- housing organisations need to prove to potential partners and consortia the relevance of housing;
- by failing to participate in such schemes, housing organisations (and more importantly their local communities) may miss out on scarce resources; and
- housing organisations must have explicit and justified strategies which cover housing and anti-poverty.

Thus a sub-theme within this chapter is how to encourage improved policy co-ordination.

There is, however, a further tension in strategic policy making and partnerships. The relationship between strategies and local communities is often ignored. Again, there is little evidence that the 'welfare to work' schemes developed in 1997 and implemented in 1998 involved local people in the planning process. Strategies were developed (and are often developed) using a top-down rather than a bottom up approach. If housing and anti-poverty strategies are to be anything more than a paper commitment, they must relate to local needs and be geared to implementation. There must be a partnership between local communities, policy makers and service deliverers.

Marian Keogh speaking at the Chartered Institute of Housing Annual Conference in 1997, questioned whether strategies work. As the Director of the **Greater Easterhouse Initiative** in Glasgow, which is involved in tackling poverty on a series of large local authority estates, she pointed out a strategy by itself does not directly tackle poverty. Instead, action is required which concentrates on what can realistically be done locally, and is relevant to local needs.

In 1995/96, the residents of Greater Easterhouse were faced with the devastating consequences of a severe freeze and sudden thaw which left many tenants with nowhere to live and with much of their furniture and personal possessions destroyed. Most of the residents did not have insurance. Anti-poverty strategies had no answer to this crisis. She concluded that the anti-poverty strategy for the city and region was irrelevant to many of the issues faced by the community.

Finally, the development and co-ordination of local strategies is often problematic because of the lack of an inter-departmental approach at the national government level and poor central-local government relationships. The Government, however, has placed considerable emphasis on policy co-ordination. The Minister for Public Health in July 1997 stressed that improvements to health 'will require a joint approach involving the Departments of Health, Environment and Transport, Education, Trade and Agriculture'. In August 1997, Peter Mandelson, Minister without Portfolio, reiterated the importance of co-ordination at national government level with the establishment of a cabinet unit to tackle poverty and social exclusion. Furthermore Hilary Armstrong, the Minster of Housing at the Chartered Institute of Public Finance and Accountancy Conference in July 1997, emphasised the need to forge a new and constructive partnership between central and local government based on the principles of democracy, local autonomy, accountability and partnership. She suggested that local authorities were at 'the sharp end of the fight against deprivation' and that

> *"... it is also about more than housing. Housing plays a critical role in the regeneration of run-down areas ... (but) that receipts should complement wider objectives such as welfare to work".*

❑ Working together

Strategic policies for tackling poverty and social exclusion are likely to be developed by a range of organisations. Apart from housing and anti-poverty strategies developed by housing organisations, there may be a broader local authority anti-poverty and/or social justice strategy. In addition, other public and voluntary sector bodies may have more targeted strategies, e.g. Education and Social Services Departments of local authorities, local health authorities, and local anti-poverty campaign groups.

Even if these organisations have not developed a strategic perspective, they may well be implementing projects and schemes that impact on anti-poverty work. The case studies in subsequent chapters identify a range of non-housing organisations who might be contributing to such work. They are summarised in Table 3.1 on page 40.

A multi-agency perspective is required which draws on the experiences, knowledge and skills of many bodies. Housing organisations, by themselves, are not likely to have the quality and quantity of in-house resources which a combination of other organisations can provide. There is no one single inter-organisational model which would ensure successful partnerships, but local anti-poverty forums are a useful starting point.

Table 3.1: Non-housing bodies and anti-poverty

LA departments	Social services Economic development Environmental health Planning Leisure and recreation
Other public sector bodies	Health authorities NHS trusts Police Training and enterprise councils
Not-for-profit bodies	Advice centres Credit unions LETS Training organisations
Private sector bodies	Building societies Other mortgage lenders
Utilities	Gas Water Electricity
Community organisations	Tenants' and residents' associations
Campaign groups	Local branches of national organisations – e.g. Shelter

Inter-organisational frameworks by themselves will not overcome the potential problems of linking together a number of anti-poverty strategies and many activities in one locality. Collaboration over policy and implementation is a beneficial and necessary activity, yet the reality is often 'a jumble of services fractionalised by professional, cultural, and organisational boundaries and by tiers of governance' (Hudson, 1987, and Webb, 1991). These problems over the co-ordination and implementation apply equally strongly to housing and community care (Lund and Foord, 1997).

Collaboration will be more effective if the following principles of public sector management are upheld:

- agreement on **roles and responsibilities** among participating agencies;
- similar or **complementary organisational structures** and functional responsibilities;
- **strong networks** of links between organisations;
- agencies can see that they will **benefit** from working together;
- **trust** that they can work together successfully – from past experiences or knowledge; and
- access to **resources** which they would not necessarily obtain by themselves.

(Hudson, 1987, and Webb, 1991)

❑ Learning from anti-poverty strategies

Local authorities have been developing anti-poverty strategies since the mid 1970s. This has been encouraged by the work of the Local Government Anti-Poverty Unit as well as the establishment of the National Local Government Forum Against Poverty. There is a wealth of experience which housing organisations (and indeed the Government) should utilise. This has been helped by the creation of an anti-poverty panel in 1997 by the Local Government Association with the remit of showcasing local authority strategies especially to the Government's social exclusion unit. Housing organisations must be aware of the scale and details of these anti-poverty strategies.

■ The scale of anti-poverty activities

In recent years, there has been a major growth in local authority action to tackle poverty. As Alcock et al (1995) indicate, there were a number of factors which contributed to this work including:

- the involvement of local authorities in central government anti-poverty programmes from the late 1960s onwards, e.g. the urban programme;
- the involvement of local authorities in competitive bidding systems for funds for urban regeneration, e.g. City Challenge and now Single Regeneration Budgets, which have enabled some emphasis to be given to anti-poverty work;
- European Union anti-poverty programmes which were launched in the mid 1970s of which there have now been three sets of initiatives – all of which have had a local dimension;

- European Union funding (through, for example, the Social Fund) for tackling aspects of social exclusion; and
- the identification of increasing levels of poverty and social exclusion at the local level in the late 1970s and early 1980s, coupled with a withdrawal of commitment by the previous government from a comprehensive welfare programme.

The types of initiatives which have developed have been extremely varied, building on the initial work by pioneering authorities such as Newcastle City Council. In the mid 1970s the Council designated priority areas and set up action teams with local funds to alleviate stress and deprivation. Many of the initiatives have thus been either area-based or service-orientated or both, e.g. welfare-benefits take-up campaigns. However, there have also been innovative attempts to develop **broader** anti-poverty strategies. Strathclyde Regional Council developed a strategy to tackle multiple deprivation as early as 1976 (Willis, 1991).

There have been a number of attempts to identify the scale of such work but surveys have suffered from recent local government reorganisation. Nevertheless, Alcock et al (1995) reported that studies showed that:

- in the mid 1980s, 12 metropolitan authorities in England and four regional councils in Scotland had or were developing anti-poverty strategies which went beyond individual service or area-based approaches; and
- by the mid 1990s, 55 local authorities were implementing an anti-poverty strategy in England and Wales, while a further 68 authorities were in the process of developing a strategy. In Scotland, it was estimated that 12 regional or district authorities had an anti-poverty strategy.

More recent research by the Local Government Anti-Poverty Unit, who carry out an annual survey of anti-poverty work, shows that in early 1997:

- over 60% of all local authorities in England, Scotland and Wales are involved in anti-poverty work with nearly 25% having formal anti-poverty strategies;
- around 80% of local authorities involved in anti-poverty work have located their activities within Chief Executive's Departments and work corporately;
- the type of work undertaken as part of formal anti-poverty strategies is strongly focused on welfare rights advice, debt and money advice, and benefit take-up;

- other activities frequently undertaken include community development work, supporting the development of credit unions, health promotion, low pay campaigns, and supporting community businesses; and
- virtually all local authorities with a formal anti-poverty strategy work in partnership with other agencies including the voluntary sector, health authorities and the Benefits Agency.

Housing organisations need to find out the scale of these past and current actions as well as participating in new ones. Anti-poverty strategies may be initiated in a wide range of disciplines and agencies. Housing organisations will have to undertake detailed local research to find out what is already happening.

■ Details of policy development

There is plenty of experience of developing general anti-poverty strategies which housing organisations must take account of in drawing up more specific policies (see, for instance, Alcock et al, 1995). The following examples illustrate different dimensions of policy development.

Central Regional Council's Social Strategy

In the 1980s, anti-poverty action had been limited mainly to welfare rights work, but in 1990 the Council decided to adopt a Social Strategy to tackle poverty and social exclusion. The strategy was developed by a joint councillor/officer working group, and included representatives from the voluntary sector. The strategy developed four key features:

- identification of deprived communities on the basis of indicators of need, utilising the 1991 small area census data;
- resource allocation, and in particular the potential for top-slicing budgets on the basis of geographical need;
- developing partnerships for policy formulation, with organisations including District Councils, but principally voluntary sector bodies; and
- decentralisation of services, management and a degree of political control to local area committees, involving local communities and politicians.

The development of this strategy illustrates four crucial aspects of the process:

- the importance of undertaking thorough and detailed research and analysis on poverty and existing policies and practices, i.e. a social audit;
- the involvement of politicians as well as officers directly in the development of policy;
- the involvement of local people and local communities in policy formulation; and
- the involvement of other organisations, especially voluntary sector bodies.

Coventry City Council and the Coventry Anti-Poverty Forum

In the early 1990s, Coventry councillors identified poverty as the single most important equal opportunities issue, and in 1993 decided to develop an anti-poverty strategy. Both officers and councillors were involved, as were other agencies and the local community. In developing the strategy, it was found that front line officers often did not feel that they were working as part of an effective and co-ordinated anti-poverty approach.

As a result of these discussions a number of initiatives were taken including:

- setting up an Anti-Poverty Forum. This has nearly 30 members including representatives from the Health Authority, Health Care Trusts, the Racial Equality Council and other voluntary sector bodies as well as councillors. It is chaired by Coventry Cathedral, with secretarial support from the City Council;
- the establishment and strengthening of the City Council's Social Justice Policy Team;
- forming an Anti-Poverty and Equality Group for councillors. This is mainly for policy co-ordination and promoting anti-poverty and equal opportunities work in all areas of the Council's activities, so that they are embedded in the overall Council's Corporate Action Plan; and
- research on key policy areas through the Anti-Poverty Forum, which so far have included, for instance, advice and information services.

Four key themes emerge from this example:

- the importance of a community-wide forum for identifying key issues and developing policies;
- the need to adopt a corporate approach so that all policies and practices are evaluated in terms of their contribution to an anti-poverty focus;
- the need to co-ordinate different local policy areas, such as anti-poverty, equal opportunities and environmental strategies such as local Agenda 21; and
- the importance of councillor commitment and involvement.

Northamptonshire County Council

Northamptonshire County Council is in the process of developing an anti-poverty strategy and an annual action plan. Each year the strategy will be reviewed and a new action plan developed. The strategy will be wide ranging, with the following features which are particularly significant in terms of good practice:

- the commitment to work with district councils, other public service bodies, voluntary organisations, private companies and local people;
- an emphasis on targeting resources to specific groups and geographical areas;
- detailed research on poverty and social exclusion, including improving understanding of the nature and extent of poverty, developing measures to enable targeting of specific initiatives, and analysing the effects of changes in government policies; and
- providing a basis for contributing to bids for resources such as the Single Regeneration Budget.

Of particular significance, in this example, is the decision to develop an annual anti-poverty strategy as a form of local policy planning, with a timetable and policy making format similar to local housing strategies and local economic development plans. This illustration also shows the importance of researching and analysing the nature of poverty and social exclusion.

Overall these three case studies suggest some valuable lessons for housing organisations in developing housing and anti-poverty strategies. These include the following four points:

- political commitment;
- corporate and partnership working;
- policy co-ordination and local policy planning; and
- the importance of information, research and analysis.

These lessons are now each examined in more detail.

■ Political commitment

The three case studies and other anti-poverty initiatives demonstrate the need for political commitment. Local authority housing (and other) committees and the boards of registered social housing landlords must be fully involved in identifying the relationship between the way the housing is provided, and poverty and social exclusion. This may be done through arrangements such as joint officer/councillor working groups or councillor run policy teams.

The method used by some local authorities, such as Coventry City Council, could be replicated by registered social landlords. Coventry uses a lead member system, where a nominated councillor or committee member acts as the focus for anti-poverty strategies. Tasks might include:

- guiding the direction of policy development and implementation;
- taking a corporate overview of co-ordination issues;
- providing a focus for the development of external relations; and
- encouraging a 'learning approach' about the nature of poverty and social exclusion.

■ Corporate and partnership working

An individual department and/or organisation approach is unlikely by itself to be effective or successful. Social housing organisations must work with other agencies and departments on anti-poverty strategies. The key issue is how to organise such initiatives successfully when working together does not happen spontaneously.

Local authorities can act as strategic enablers, co-ordinating the strategy, and incorporating the housing dimension through the participation of a range of housing organisations. A more common approach is to set up an **anti-poverty**

forum, based on the equal participation of a wide range of public, private, voluntary sector and local community organisations, including local authority housing departments and registered social landlords – as happens in Coventry, Leicester and Wakefield. In the latter, the anti-poverty forum established by the Council is setting up working groups on specific projects such as advocacy and advice and welfare benefits.

■ Policy co-ordination and local policy planning

The development of an annual anti-poverty strategy by local authorities has many advantages, including:

- focusing regular attention on poverty and social exclusion;
- encouraging other departments and organisations to review and evaluate their policies and practices;
- promoting a more co-ordinated approach – thus avoiding duplication or conflicting initiatives;
- providing a basis for bidding for resources such as SRB; and
- helping to improve the performance of contributing organisations in the eyes of monitoring and regulatory bodies.

Nevertheless there are two **pitfalls** to avoid:

- **duplication** – when poverty is addressed in other local policy plans, such as housing strategies, housing investment programmes, urban renewal strategies, community care plans, local economic development strategies, local Agenda 21 plans, home energy conservation plans and local plans under the Town and Country Planning Acts; and
- **marginalisation** – because they do not flow from a statutory requirement, anti-poverty strategies may not get allocated the necessary resources.

However, the experience of those who have done it is that an anti-poverty strategy is essential in drawing attention to poverty and social exclusion. In addition, it helps the participating organisations to understand how poverty affects their own work and what they can do in response.

■ Research and analysis

The identification of the nature and scale of poverty and social exclusion is a vital part of the process. A good example of this is the recent study by the London Research Centre (1996) which found in London that:

- 60% of tenants in social housing have incomes below £7,500 a year;
- over 20% of households have gross incomes of less than £125 a week;
- over 70% of lone parents are in the social housing rented sector;
- nearly 20% of the population are dependent on income support compared to 10% five years ago; and
- 45% of new housing association tenants were unemployed in 1995/96 compared to 25% in 1990/91.

Comprehensive research and analysis is a vital part of the policy making process. Social housing organisations can contribute by providing in-house data and existing research. Local housing needs studies are probably the best example of this type of input – especially where there has been a focus on household incomes and housing affordability. For instance, a housing needs study for the Bradford Housing Forum on Race and Housing provided clear evidence of poverty, and 'in many ways the central findings had nothing to do with housing' (Ratcliffe, 1996). Among Pakistani and Bangladeshi households, for instance, as many as half contained no one in full time work.

❑ Strategic policy making process

The process of developing housing and anti-poverty strategies requires housing organisations to make use of their existing skills in policy making and strategic management. Housing organisations should be familiar with the basic principles through their involvement, for instance, in local policy planning initiatives such as local housing strategies and in business planning.

Stages in the planning process:

- initial research and information;
- identifying the problems and issues;
- setting aims and objectives;
- generating alternative strategies;
- evaluating alternative strategies;
- selecting the most appropriate strategy;
- implementation; and
- monitoring and evaluation.

This model of the policy making process can be applied to any situation. Housing organisations frequently use this framework in drawing up business plans. The Chartered Institute of Housing *Good Practice Guide* on business planning contains detailed guidance and examples (Catterick, 1995). Similarly, the Audit Commission (1992) and the Chartered Institute of Housing (1997) have both published good practice briefings on how local authorities should develop local housing strategies. The Chartered Institute of Housing and the Local Government Association are due to publish a major new guide to Local Housing Strategies in April 1998. The same principles can be applied to housing and anti-poverty strategies. The following subsections focus on examples of important aspects of some of the key stages.

■ Initial research and information

Generally there is a lack of information on low incomes at a district level. Official government statistics are either not available or are unreliable at the local scale. Housing departments and housing associations may have some of this information, collected particularly at the start of tenancies to assess benefit eligibility, and in some cases as part of registering applications.

Local housing needs surveys, as part of the assessment of aggregate housing requirements, may also contain relevant information. Most surveys are primarily focused on issues of housing and affordability, and thus collect household data on incomes. These studies generally underestimate the extent of household income because they rarely seek data on personal savings, and some respondents are reluctant to provide income information.

However, initial research and information collection is not just about obtaining objective external data on poverty and social exclusion. It also raises more fundamental issues such as:

- **definition and measurement** of poverty and social exclusion. These issues are considered in detail in the appendices to this Guide as well as in the next section, but research sometimes makes false assumptions. An example of this is the view that poverty is concentrated on large council housing estates. However, research by Lee and Murie (1997) showed that that policies based on this perspective would ignore, for instance, ethnic minority communities living in older unimproved housing in inner areas; and
- **new approaches to needs studies**. Housing organisations ought to consider making use of research approaches which draw on innovative practices from public and social policy such as community profiling and social audits – both of which involve local communities. Urban housing authorities could adapt the approach of parish appraisal studies in rural areas – some of which have focused on rural housing and poverty problems.

Finally, as was pointed out in Chapter 1, housing organisations ought to 'take stock' of themselves at this stage of the process. This should involve an audit of the way they have an impact on poverty – by examining what they do, and how they do it.

Problem and issue identification

A significant aspect is the analysis of the local geographical patterns of poverty. Lack of local income data presents difficulties, but many organisations make use of a variety of poverty-related indicators. These might include, for example, the following poverty and deprivation indices:

- Department of Environment's **Index of Local Conditions**, which is now the official deprivation index, and is used to allocate resources at a local authority level. It consists of 13 variables including unemployment, children in low income earning households, housing lacking basic amenities, and income support recipients;
- **Townsend Index** (or 'z' score) which consists of four variables – households without access to a car, households not in owner occupation, households in overcrowded living conditions, and unemployment; and
- **Breadline Britain Index** which consists of six variables including households containing a person with a limiting long term illness, unskilled workers, and lone parent families.

Details of these indices can be found in Gordon and Forrest (1993 and 1995) who point out that at the local authority level in England the choice of indices has relatively little effect on the results. Of the 10 local authorities which exhibit the highest levels of deprivation using the Index of Local Conditions, seven of them are in the top 10 of both the Townsend Index and the Breadline Britain Index.

At the intra-authority level (e.g. ward and enumeration district level), the choice of indicators is more significant because variables which include tenure-related measures can have a significant impact on the results. Ward and enumeration district boundaries may themselves not be particularly relevant, as they do not reflect the nature of local communities. Such difficulties can be overcome particularly through the use of Geographical Information Systems (GIS) which can also be used to manipulate large amounts of geographically-based data for poverty and deprivation studies.

Scottish Homes operates the most sophisticated GIS for housing purposes in the UK.

In the **West Midlands**, Birmingham City Council is working with the Housing Corporation on making more effective use of existing information sources for analysing housing needs.

In the **East Midlands**, a consortium of three local authorities (Leicester City Council, Harborough District Council and East Northamptonshire District Council), two universities (De Montfort University and Leicester University) and a consultant are exploring the potential of GIS for housing needs and affordability studies.

A number of local authorities, for instance, produce poverty profiles:

Stockport Borough Council

In March 1997, Stockport Borough Council published the latest of a series of poverty profiles. The report draws attention to disadvantaged groups in neighbourhoods so as first to stimulate action in areas of greatest need, second to act as a baseline for evaluating the authority's anti-poverty action plan, and third to provide information to the Council and other organisations for use in bidding for resources.

The poverty profile draws together information on a wide range of topics including unemployment, benefit receipts, poor housing, mortgage repossession, health, educational attainment, ethnicity, and gender. Analysis was carried out at a borough, ward and enumeration district level.

The study concluded that 1 in 6 households in the local authority area were living in poverty. It also found that all wards except one had at least one enumeration district considered to be relatively deprived, and that while the highest concentrations of poverty are in a small number of wards, the majority of poor households live **outside** those wards.

The findings have thus raised important policy issues including:

- the appropriateness of targeting action on an area-basis;
- the need to ensure that policies are developed and implemented which meet the needs of **all** households in poverty in Stockport; and
- the importance of a multi-agency approach.

■ Establishing aims and objectives

As the three case studies in the previous section showed, a vital aspect of this stage of the policy making process is the joint involvement of officers and councillors. The establishment of overall aims is not only crucial for subsequent stages in the process, but it is also important to establish a culture within the organisation which supports the objectives of a housing and anti-poverty strategy.

Much of the literature on business planning (e.g. Catterick, 1995) highlights that objectives must be SMART (Specific, Measurable, Achievable, Realistic, and Timed). Therefore, a broad commitment to reduce a specific symptom of poverty, such as ensuring that all households on a social housing estate gain entitlement to a range of welfare benefits, is not satisfactory. More precision is needed on – which benefits? and, what timescale?

■ Strategy identification and selection

Having identified aims and objectives, the next stage in the process is the identification of strategies – how will the housing organisation get to where it wants to be in relation to anti-poverty policies? Catterick (1995) suggests that one method of identifying strategies is to focus attention on three issues:

- **what must we do?** e.g. statutory requirements;
- **what can we not do?** e.g. legal constraints; and
- **what can we do?** e.g. the degree of autonomy and choice for the organisation.

The relevance of this approach can be illustrated by reference to the role of registered social landlords. A number of housing associations have shown considerable interest in the American equivalent of community development corporations (see, for example, Bowman, 1995), which are involved in not only the provision of social rented housing but also employment and education initiatives. In Britain, legislation restricts the range of activities. Wider actions have to be subsidiary to the main housing function.

Having developed a range of strategies, the next stage involves the evaluation and selection of the most appropriate approaches, by testing them against consistent criteria. Catterick suggests four criteria which can be applied to **any** strategic policy making situation – including a housing and anti-poverty policy:

- **acceptability** – which strategies are councillors and officers willing to support?

- **feasibility** – can the strategies be implemented in terms of the resource envelope?
- **suitability** – do the strategies fit in with the other role of the housing organisation?
- **cultural fit** – do the strategies tie in with organisational culture?

Research and information, problem identification and issue analysis, establishing aims and objectives, and strategy identification and selection are vital stages in the policy making process. The implementation of specific projects which would form part of a strategy for action is dealt with in Chapters 4-6. The important but neglected issues of resources and monitoring and evaluation are considered in Chapter 7.

A recurring theme throughout this chapter is that policy making is not simply a technical matter, and therefore the next section considers organisational and political issues.

❑ Organisational frameworks

The previous section has primarily focused on how housing organisations should develop housing and anti-poverty strategies. But other organisations, particularly local government, may have developed broader anti-poverty initiatives. A housing department and housing committee developing a housing-orientated anti-poverty approach will need to be linked to the wider strategies of the authority. Similarly, a registered social landlord may be keen to develop anti-poverty initiatives, but will need to liaise with local authorities, other housing associations and voluntary sector bodies.

Housing organisations must appreciate the multi-agency approach which is required for anti-poverty strategies. This requires collaboration at all stages of the policy making process. They need to become involved, as in the three earlier case studies, in local anti-poverty forums and networks.

Finally, there is the need to involve communities and local people in developing anti-poverty strategies. Local anti-poverty forums and networks are a useful mechanism for achieving this.

Housing organisations may develop anti-poverty strategies as part of internal strategic management. Unfortunately, this can result in a paternalistic approach which treats those in poverty as merely deserving of charity. Worse, it misses out on the ideas and skills of local people who need to be part of the policy making process. Even on what may first appear to be a problem estate with a high level of community breakdown, there is likely to be an untapped reservoir of ideas. Gibson's work on 'planning for real' has shown the capacity of communities around the country (Gibson, 1993 and 1997) to contribute both the definition of problems, and development of solutions.

In Scotland, community based anti-poverty initiatives have a longer history and are more common. They include in Glasgow, for example, the development of community-based housing associations involving local resident control in the inner city areas. These had been so successful by the early 1990s that the 28 community based housing associations had modernised nearly 16,000 houses (Scottish Homes, 1991). Also, in Glasgow, in relation to public sector renewal, the City Council has developed a community ownership programme for parts of six of its largest estates which include the encouragement of housing co-operatives (Clapham et al, 1991). Some of the community based associations provide shop or workshop space. Others have welfare rights, or community work, staff.

❑ Housing and anti-poverty strategies

This chapter has focused attention on the process of developing a housing and anti-poverty strategy. The following three examples illustrate the progress which has been made.

Moat Housing Society anti-poverty strategy

Moat Housing Society is an association managing 3000 rented homes scattered across eight counties in South East England. It is a member of a group structure, with an anti-poverty strategy, which recognises that the association is not a major stakeholder in any single community.

The strategy developed from the welfare rights service offered by the association. The service initially established to offer advice, adapted as demands grew during the 1990s. The focus switched with a greater emphasis being placed on training and resourcing other staff to deliver benefits advice.

By the mid 1990s the association recognised, from survey data, a growing level of benefit dependency and falling average incomes. To continue solely with benefits advice on demand was not sufficient; a more proactive approach was required.

A series of individual initiatives were launched to tackle the main sources of tenant income (benefits and low paid employment) and expenditure (rent, fuel, furniture, and crisis expenditure). On the income side the benefits service undertook proactive work with benefits road shows, take up campaigns and improving access to benefits information. On the expenditure side it developed energy advice to assist all residents in controlling their fuel usage, offered furnished tenancies, established a Tenant Fund to help with crisis costs, and developed information packs for households coping with death, a new baby or change in employment status.

A second phase of the strategy is beginning to develop more estate based solutions, in partnership with residents and individual local authorities.

Portsmouth City Council

Portsmouth is a city with a population of 190,000. Following the review of local government during the mid 1990s it gained unitary status in 1997. The Council's strategy has been based on a detailed assessment of need derived from the census and other sources, with priorities being set through resident surveys, and customer focus groups. The surveys brought some interesting results. Residents indicated that job creation was a major priority for the Council, as were helping the elderly and tackling crime. All three featured above housing. A comparison of data between the two survey years 1993 and 1995 also reveals changing trends, with housing's priority falling and being overtaken by a call to address the needs of all people on low incomes.

Having previously run take up campaigns and other poverty initiatives the Council committed itself to a city wide strategy. The strategy combines individual Council initiatives and the voluntary sector – by requiring voluntary groups applying for Council grants to address poverty issues in their projects.

The Council's own initiatives include continuing its debt advice and benefit take up campaigns. It has also built links between the central poverty team and other service departments, including housing and leisure. The former has resulted in additional grants for loft insulation, while the latter has enabled the extension of out of school activities. The Council also supports the formation of Credit Unions, and forums to exchange good practice on debt and benefits.

Birmingham City Council social justice strategies

Birmingham City Council is developing a social justice strategy and uses the term to recognise that poverty extends beyond financial issues into wider inequality. A social justice strategy is defined as 'a multi-agency strategy whereby inequality between income groups within the locality is reduced, participation in all aspects of society by lower income and socially excluded groups is increased and social cohesion is enhanced'. Such a strategy will:

- involve joint working between various agencies in the community;
- generate decentralisation to local agencies and community groups;
- resource, train and involve local people in projects which stimulate local employment and a sense of community; and
- actively encourage self help solutions.

Birmingham developed its corporate anti-poverty strategy in 1992, after several years of individual departmental strategies and initiatives. The corporate strategy set a 3 year programme of activities, which built on individual department initiatives. The 1992 strategy resulted in:

- a review of billing and debt recovery practices;
- enhanced advice services;
- improvements in access to healthy food;
- improvements in employment advice;
- reviews of service accessibility;
- monitoring utilities practices; and
- improving understanding of poverty within the City.

The Council is reviewing its corporate strategy based on a broader concept of poverty, and tackling both poverty and inequality. This broader definition covers social exclusion, aiming to ensure all citizens can participate in the economic, social, political and cultural life of the city. The review also examines the role of other agencies.

The five years of corporate anti-poverty work and research have provided an understanding of the scale and dispersal of poverty within the city. The review is seeking to build on these lessons and recognises effective action requires:

- a co-ordinated multi-disciplinary approach that addresses the economic, social, cultural and environmental aspects of social exclusion;
- a strategic approach which places issues of social exclusion and poverty at the centre of the organisation's policy and budget decision making processes;
- local partnerships to maximise resources and action;
- civic leadership by the City Council to promote social justice; and
- bottom up approaches which involve people in developing solutions to poverty, social exclusion, empowerment and community development.

In its framework document the Council has identified a series of basic principles to guide the strategic development process. These are:

- targeting services and resources to areas and people in poverty;
- making sure economic and social regeneration benefits people in greatest need, and is holistic and sustainable;
- improving access to council services;
- enabling participation by people living in poverty;
- maximising incomes of people living in poverty;
- minimising the occurrence of debt; and
- tackling discrimination and inequality.

The strategy has been developed through extensive consultation with service departments to identify areas of action. While strong on its broader approach to poverty, through social exclusion, the strategy is weaker on partnership and the enabling role of co-ordinating the voluntary and other agencies which operate across the city impacting on the lives of citizens. This aspect is likely to be developed next.

While there are limits to the commitment of utilities or voluntary organisations in any local authority area, the local authority has a lot of influence. It is a major funder, has influence over planning, and represents the area to external bodies and regulators. Local authorities, as strategic enablers, can bring together agencies and focus collective attention on the theme of social justice.

The themes identified in these case studies provide the context for the specific activities and elements in an anti-poverty approach. They are:

- a strategy is essential for raising the profile for the wider issues of poverty and social exclusion;
- a strategy forms the basis for specific actions;
- specific initiatives need to be part of a multi-agency partnership; and
- elements of an anti-poverty strategy are essential as part of an advocacy and campaigning role to tackle poverty.

Guide to further reading

The development of anti-poverty strategies

One of the most useful guides on this general topic is:

Alcock P et al (1995): *Combating Local Poverty – The Management of Anti-Poverty Strategies by Local Government*: Luton, LGMB

The policy and strategy making process

The most useful material are guides to business planning and local housing strategy formulation and they include:

Audit Commission (1992): *Developing Local Authority Housing Strategies*: London, HMSO

Catterick P (1995): *Business Planning for Housing*: Coventry, CIH

Chartered Institute of Housing (1997): *Good Practice Briefing No 7 – Local Housing Strategies*: Coventry, CIH

Community profiling and social audits

Burton P (1993): *Community Profiling*: Bristol, School for Advanced Urban Studies

Hawtin M et al (1994): *Community Profiling*: Buckingham, Open University Press

Percy-Smith J Ed (1996): *Needs Assessments in Public Policy*: Buckingham, Open University Press

Chapter 4

Housing Management and Anti-Poverty Initiatives

This chapter describes and analyses anti-poverty initiatives which focus on the core activity of housing management, under the following headings:

- benefit advice;
- money management advice;
- pre-tenancy counselling;
- debt recovery;
- rent and affordability strategies;
- furniture schemes;
- hardship funds;
- home contents insurance; and
- role of concierges and caretakers.

Case studies have been selected to show wide ranging ideas developed by housing organisations within a strategic framework.

❑ Benefit advice

Many people are poorer than they need to be because they do not claim the welfare benefits they are entitled to. The levels of non-take up are particularly high for some benefits. It has been estimated that the take up of national means tested benefits is 90% for housing benefit, 80% for Income Support and 64% for Family Credit (Kempson, 1994).

Table 4.1: Non-take up of benefits

Benefit	Range of non-take up (%)	Range of entitled non-recipients (000)	Average amount unclaimed (£/week)
Housing benefit	4–12	200–600	21.45
Council tax benefit	20–29	1,340–2,170	5.45
Family credit	20	180	24.00
Income support	12–21	720–1,390	22.85

Source: DSS (1995) *Income Related Benefits – Estimates of Take Up in 1993/94*: London, DSS

Welfare benefits advice is the bedrock of housing management activity in addressing poverty. With high levels of benefits dependency among local authority and association tenants, this is central to any strategy. In many instances, housing organisations have employed welfare benefits advisers or have trained their staff in benefits advice to maximise rent collection. Staff who ensure housing benefits are claimed correctly, can also help the household by reviewing other benefit entitlement.

Welfare benefits advice is **not** restricted to simple one-to-one advice delivered through a reactive service. It can also take a proactive approach, such as:

- benefits road shows taking the message to town centres and estates;
- estate surgeries offering appointments on an estate or in a sheltered scheme; and
- take up campaigns.

The impact can be dramatic. Advice staff in Strathclyde increased take up by £5 million a year (Willis, 1991). In York a take up campaign costing £10,000, yielded £60,000 in increased benefits. And, a strategy by the former West Glamorgan County Council in 1993 yielded £500,000 (Local Government Information Unit, 1995). In Coventry in 1995/96 welfare benefit take up worth £6 million were achieved through the free advice service, at a cost to the City Council of £0.8 million.

South Lanarkshire Council has a benefits advice service offering a one stop shop approach on all finance matters. It has five staff drawn from housing, welfare rights, and finance. One reason for setting up this unit in 1996 was to improve the take up of welfare benefits – in the case of council tax benefits, the take-up rate was only 28%.

In addition to the office service, there is a free phone service plus home visits for those unable to visit the office or phone. The Council has liaised with other agencies in respect of providing joint surgeries on outlying estates, sheltered housing schemes and residential care homes. This proactive approach has brought significant benefits, as small weekly increases have made material differences to individuals' standards of living.

Incomes have been increased by over £2 million per annum. The benefits advice unit identified over 3,000 tenants who were claiming housing benefit but not council tax benefit for which they were also entitled. Rent arrears have also been reduced, with fewer court actions and associated costs and tenant distress.

As part of the process of checking entitlement to housing benefit, officers at **East Northamptonshire District Council** are able to identify whether households are eligible for and claiming family credit. If a household appears to be eligible but not claiming, the District Council informs both the Family Credit Unit of the Benefits Agency and the household in writing. On average 150 letters are sent in a year.

It is essential that a multi-agency approach is adopted on welfare advice. Many local authorities have welfare rights units which provide a diverse range of services. Stockport Metropolitan Borough Council's Welfare Rights Unit includes, for instance, staff dedicated to specific geographical areas, hospital welfare rights and benefits advisers, community care welfare officers, debt counsellors, and county court caseworkers. Social housing providers **must** liaise with such units, to maximise effectiveness and avoid duplication of effort.

❑ Money management advice

For households with tight financial budgets, money management skills are vital for survival. Households often raid budgets, such as food, to pay for unforeseen events which may force them in to debt. Debt is strongly correlated to low income. Households with a net income of less than £100 per week are only 11% of all households, but represent 40% of all household debts. With an estimated 0.5 million households in multiple debt, owing money to more than three creditors, there has been a growth in demand for money management advice. This often takes the form of debt counselling, which deals with the current crisis, and is likely to lead to more general money advice.

One of the leading agencies on money advice is the Birmingham Settlement. It however is not alone, with around 500 other agencies in the UK offering advice, ranging from local authority based services to independent charities and advice centres (Kempson, 1995).

The Birmingham Settlement is a multi-purpose charity based in inner city Birmingham. It has pioneered a broad range of advice services over the past 20 years, ranging from community training and employment projects to national debt advice lines. Its advice services are free, impartial and confidential.

The Settlement runs a National Debtline, offering advice to individual callers from across the UK. The service receives over 60,000 calls a year, and compiles a computerised record of each case call, so callers are more quickly and easily dealt with and do not rely on a worker having to write or review hand-written case notes.

A Business Debtline was launched in 1992. This offers telephone advice to self employed people and businesses who are starting up. As the demand for this service continues to increase, the Settlement is aiming to help others to set up Business Debtline franchises elsewhere in the UK.

The money advice is centred around negotiating with creditors realistic repayment schedules, based upon amounts clients can afford, while still allowing for unexpected costs.

❑ Pre-tenancy counselling

This element of a strategy may sit within welfare benefits advice, but the approach is not restricted to benefits advice and includes affordability and tenancy rights.

In the past tenancies were viewed lightly. The signing up process, where a tenant entered into the tenancy, may have been undertaken by a support member of staff, and be little more than signing a sheet at a reception counter and collecting the key. This approach trivialises the value and importance of a tenancy.

At sign up, housing officers, should go through the tenancy details to ensure the tenant understands his rights and responsibilities in each clause. The rent clause provides an opportunity to discuss any entitlement to housing benefit. For first time householders, a discussion about other household costs (including gas, electricity and water) may help them in thinking about the total cost of running a home. An income and expenditure budget statement can help personal financial planning.

Many associations and local authorities follow good practice in this area – including Taff Housing Association with its pre-tenancy counselling, and Chester City Council who send benefits advice staff to all new housing association developments to help with sign ups and housing benefit claims (CIH, 1996). Indeed, some local authorities publicise the availability of pre-tenancy determinations to find out if housing benefit will cover the rent before the tenant signs the tenancy agreement and encourage potential claimants to take up this option.

❑ Debt recovery

Dealing with debt, particularly rent arrears, is a major feature of housing management. Other services within an organisation can lead tenants into debt, and the organisation should have a corporate policy on debt recovery which ensures sensitive recovery practices. The recent Chartered Institute of Housing publication, *Recovering Housing Debt: A Legal Guide* is the most comprehensive guide available to the relevant issues.

Leicester City Council has adopted a Fair Debt Collection Strategy, as part of its corporate anti-poverty strategy, to ensure consistent practices across the Council towards debt collection (Leicester City Council, 1996a). The strategy forms part of a wider anti-poverty strategy adopted by the Council. It is based on a series of principles:

- people have a responsibility to pay;
- collection services should be efficient and sensitive;
- the prime issue in collection is the debtors ability to pay;
- repayment agreements must take account of the needs of dependants;
- most Council debts are priority debts, and will usually take precedence over other debts;
- a fair balance should be achieved between competing creditors; and
- recovery will be both proactive and reactive .

The Council's code of practice commits it to sensitive recovery practices including translation facilities, use of plain language, advice and a flexible approach regarding arrears repayments in recognition of different individual circumstances.

The Council also has a corporate procedure for debt recovery, which includes a repayment calculation table. The table uses disposable income to calculate repayments for a debt, thus taking account of dependants and other financial commitments.

Arrears Repayment Table (Figures in £)

Disposable Income	*Repayment per Week*
0	4.80
0 – 19.99	5.10
20 – 24.99	6.00
25 – 29.99	10.00

For each additional £5 of disposal income repayment increases by £2.

❑ Rent and affordability strategies

Affordability has become a prominent issue for housing associations and their stakeholders, because of rent increases above inflation, resulting from declining capital subsidies since 1988. The CORE (COntinuous REcording) system developed jointly by the National Housing Federation and the Housing Corporation provides information on long term trends in England.

Table 4.2: NHF CORE rent and income indices

Base (Q.1)	Rents All lettings	Income Workers	Income Non-workers
1989	100.0	100.0	100.0
1990	115.2	111.4	104.1
1991	130.3	119.4	112.9
1992	146.5	125.8	121.9
1993	163.3	131.3	130.8
1994	172.6	133.5	137.8
1995	184.1	137.3	141.6
1996	193.0	141.3	150.2
1996 (Q.3)	200.3	148.3	153.4

Source: NHF *CORE Lettings Bulletin*

The most recent evidence from CORE suggests a slowing down of the rate of increase. This could be due to a recognition of affordability concerns by associations, pressure from housing benefit changes or pressure from the inclusion of rent information in bidding for capital grants.

There are marked differences both in rent levels, and in the way they have changed, between England, Scotland and Wales – reflecting national variations in government priorities.

Table 4.3: Average weekly rents – 2 bed housing association property (£)

Year	England	Scotland	Wales
1993	46.30	27.85	42.50
1994	48.07	28.33	43.26
1995	50.80	29.46	43.00
1996	52.05	30.89	42.95

Table 4.4: Average local authority and housing association weekly rents (£)

	England		Scotland		Wales	
Year	LA	HA	LA	HA	LA	HA
1990	23.76	28.97	20.91	21.00	23.49	30.04
1994	35.90	45.90	27.79	27.85	34.11	43.00

Housing association rents have risen steeply, but in Wales they have levelled off partly because of Tai Cymru's attempts since 1993 to seek (first) a voluntary rent freeze, (second) competitive rent bidding, and (third) benchmarking, described in Chapter 2. In Scotland, although rents have increased sharply, they started from a much lower base. Table 4.4 shows that there is very little difference in local authority and housing association rents in Scotland, and they have increased at the same rate.

The NHF, the SFHA and the WFHA have all contributed to the affordability debate, while recognising the difficulty of establishing a measure due to rapid change. Under its 1996 policy, the NHF stated that:

> *"Rents are affordable if the majority of working households taking up new tenancies are not caught in the poverty trap (because of dependency on housing benefit) or paying more than 25% of their net income on rent".*

The policy applies to stock collectively, rather than individuals. And it only applies to new lettings, rather than relets, and it excludes non-working households, where rent is covered by housing benefit. The policy allows indicator rents to be calculated for various property types. The WFHA definition of affordability is similar to that of the NHF, but comparisons with Scotland are difficult because of a different approach. Nevertheless, the key points on affordability levels are:

- in England, nearly 70% of cases failed the affordability test;
- in Wales, 63% of working households failed the affordability test; and
- in Scotland, only 28% of working households failed the SFHA test.

Affordability is not just a national issue, because rents are crucial in **local** examination of poverty. While housing costs are often the largest single item of expenditure for a working household, few associations have, however, used affordability considerations as a key variable in setting their rent policies. The main variables have been cost based for each development, or more recently expenditure based. Examples of associations operating explicit affordability policies have been provided in Chapter 2.

❑ Furniture schemes

For new households taking up a tenancy, furniture, or lack of it, can be a major problem. Under the DSS Social Fund regulations, a claimant may qualify for a loan only in certain specific circumstances. The loan is repaid through deductions from weekly means-tested benefits. This can increase poverty, and contribute to multiple debt problems.

A variety of furniture schemes have, therefore, been set up by local authorities, often working with voluntary agencies, and by housing associations.

Salford City Council and furnished flats

This project sets out both to help young people who cannot afford to buy furniture, and to tackle the problem of low demand for council flats in some areas. The aim is to have 450 furnished flats by Spring 1998, so that people adversely affected by the welfare and benefits system can access self-contained long term furnished accommodation.

Furnished flats are offered in four housing management areas, in one and two bedroom properties, in both high rise and low rise schemes. The flats are either fully or part furnished. Fully furnished includes – a large dining table and four chairs, a two seater settee, fridge, cooker, bed with headboard, double wardrobe, chest of drawers, lampshades, carpets, curtains, and a start up pack of bedding and kitchen utensils. Part furnished includes – a fridge, cooker, carpets and curtains.

The cost for tenants is a service charge of between £12.55 and £19.76 a week which is eligible for housing benefit. The furniture is bought out of the housing revenue account, which also pays for the administration and staffing costs. It is estimated that the scheme will be self financing after five years.

Associations, with more scattered stock, have opted to offer tenancies on furnished or unfurnished terms. This gives each incoming household a choice, and often within the scheme there is the facility to select a part furnished tenancy, with the tenant adding the items they already own.

Notting Hill Housing Trust is a London-based association managing 10,000 tenancies predominantly across West London. The Trust is a keen advocate of furnished tenancies, and currently manages more than 1,000 of them. Tenants are offered a choice of tenancy, furnished or unfurnished, and a choice of items. The rent is adjusted to cover the cost of the items selected by the tenant, and a furnished tenancy agreement detailing the items provided is entered into by the tenant.

The furniture remains the Trust's property, and this along with the enforceable nature of the weekly service charge included in the tenancy agreement, means that the charge is eligible for housing benefit. The range of items is extensive, but the majority of tenants opt for a package that on average adds £13 per week to the rent. This may include a fridge, cooker, sofa and double bed.

The scheme is self financing. The capital costs of the items are totalled and depreciated over four years, with allowances made for interest, administration, insurance and write-offs associated with damage.

Weekly cost of typical items	
Double bed and headboard	£0.74
Three piece suite	£1.52
Gas cooker (including connection)	£2.28
Carpets for 3 bed unit	£2.50
Curtains for 3 bed unit	£1.53

❑ Hardship funds

Following the changes to the DSS grants, and the cash limited budget to fund repayable loans, a small number of housing associations operate a grant system for their tenants. Schemes offer cash to meet unforeseen or emergency costs. The grant is usually only available after the tenant has applied for other sources of funding, and has a maximum limit.

Payments have covered items such as a new pair of shoes for a child; a smart skirt, blouse and shoes for a tenant who had got a job but could not afford to buy new work clothes; and gardening equipment where a tenant with children transferred to a house with a large garden.

However, even for housing associations which operate such funds, their impact will be limited, and if widely publicised may raise false expectations. Most associations operate the funds internally and rely upon referrals from front line staff, with the assessment being carried out by the welfare benefits team.

The **Gwalia Housing Group** manages 2,500 homes predominantly in South Wales. Its tenants' welfare fund makes one-off payments in cases of extreme hardship. One of its aims is to improve acceptance rates on offers of accommodation. The fund helps, for instance, tenants to buy key items of furniture. It thus reduces the risk of debts and helps to sustain the tenancy. The fund is a last resort. Tenants are expected to have applied to the Social Fund and been refused and this is one of a number of eligibility tests which staff use.

Cambridge Housing Society began a scheme in mid 1997 which falls between a credit union and a hardship fund. It is a guarantee fund and is known as the 'new horizons and loan' scheme. The Society deposited a lump sum with the Cambridge Building Society and tenants will be able to borrow without security after they have made regular deposits. The aim is to give tenants access to traditional forms of finance and avoid credit sharks.

❑ Home contents insurance

For households on low incomes, insurance of personal effects can be a low priority due to the high cost of insurance. On some social housing estates household insurance is not available. To overcome these problems an increasing number of registered social landlords are offering home contents insurance policies to tenants, following the lead set by local authorities in the 1970s.

The policies cover a large number of homes, traditionally with the main premium paid by the landlord. The total policy cost plus the landlord's administration costs are then divided between tenants as individual premiums. The premiums are collected along with the rent, offering a further saving in administration.

As many low income households have less to insure, the total sum insurable is usually lower than the minimum levels required in policies available in the insurance market, which is also a benefit for small or poor households. The premiums are substantially below those available elsewhere. Aberdeen City Council offers insurance to its tenants, with a special deal for tenants over 60, who pay 56p a week for £7000 cover.

The take up of schemes varies, with most reporting 10%-20% of tenants taking up the option. The success of take up depends on the promotion campaign and the value of the scheme compared with market prices. Most schemes are marketed as landlord run, which increases confidence, but on the downside can lead to problems if the insurers are reluctant or slow to pay out. This leaves the landlord in a position of responsibility in the eyes of the tenant, but without power, for instance, to determine claims.

There are issues to resolve for such a scheme:

- will the scheme be marketed as that of the landlord or the insurance company?
- who will collect premiums?
- if the premiums are included in the rent payment and the account is in arrears, is the person insured? and
- who will process which part of the claim?

North British Housing Association are a national association operating through a regional structure. They manage 35,000 tenancies across England. North British operates a new for old home insurance scheme for tenants, with no excess. The present arrangements are through Legal and General with a policy which covers household goods and personal effects belonging to the tenant.

The policy offers householders £9,000 of cover, with a maximum pay out of £1,000 on any single item at an average cost of 31p per week. This is considerably below standard policy costs which often specify £15,000 as a minimum cover. The premiums are collected along with the weekly rent.

Claims are initially dealt with by the housing officer. If the claim exceeds £1,000 a loss adjuster is appointed. The administration of the policy is dealt with from the Head Office of the association based in Preston who monitor the claims.

The scheme has proved popular with tenants, with over 2,000 tenants using the insurance scheme.

❑ Role of concierges and caretakers

Concierges and caretakers are frequently the first point of contact between tenants and housing organisations. Their role has changed and developed substantially over the last decade not just in the UK, but also in countries such as France, the Netherlands and Sweden. In general terms, their activities are no longer primarily focused on basic cleaning and environmental maintenance, but they have become more central to core housing management activities including:

- advisory and help roles;
- good neighbour function;
- repairs reporting and minor repairs work; and
- security including liaison with police.

Although these activities do not directly tackle financial poverty, they all assist those on the lowest incomes, and are significant in helping to alleviate community breakdown (Power, 1991). The Chartered Institute of Housing's *Good Practice Briefing Taking Care of Estates* emphasises that:

> *"Caretaking and estate services are fundamental aspects of the landlord's role which affect the quality of life on estates and residents' enjoyment of home and neighbourhood"* (CIH, 1997).

In both the Netherlands and Sweden, there has been considerable interest in enhancing the role of caretakers. This is partly a response to changing social behaviour and composition of housing estates – resulting in similar concerns to those in the UK, such as community breakdown, anti-social behaviour, and more generally conflicting life styles among tenants. One of the initiatives which has been developed is an enhanced role for caretakers (or superintendents) who now have both a greater policing and security function as well as good neighbour and conflict resolution functions.

The Chartered Institute of Housing's Good Practice Briefing *Taking Care of Estates* illustrates a wide range of models and activities for an enhanced caretaking service including:

- appointing tenants as caretakers in return for a small salary or rent free accommodation;
- establishing a mobile caretaking team;
- using on-site residential caretakers; and
- developing the concept of multi-skilled caretakers.

The latter has been developed by the Peabody Trust so that their services are more responsive to local community needs. As well as traditional duties, their caretakers are also expected to undertake minor repairs and carry out redecorating tasks in certain circumstances.

'Regies de quartiers' are a French innovation which take these ideas a step further (Saunders, 1997). These are organisations which employ local residents on a part time and/or short contracts to deliver a range of services including cleaning, grounds maintenance, and minor repairs. They depend on the co-operation and support of social housing landlords who are their principal client. Saunders suggests that these types of 'resident services organisations' could potentially be useful in estate regeneration.

Guide to further reading

Housing management core activities

CIH (1996): *Housing Standards Management Manual*: Coventry, CIH
CIH (various): *Good Practice Briefing Notes*: Coventry, CIH
CIH (1997): *Recovering Housing Debt: A Legal Guide*: Coventry, CIH

CHAPTER 5

HOUSING DEVELOPMENT AND ANTI-POVERTY INITIATIVES

This chapter investigates how some of the core activities of housing development can be utilised as part of an anti-poverty approach. It illustrates, through case studies, what can be achieved and focuses on four topics:

- affordability and housing development;
- energy efficiency;
- estate redevelopment; and
- community involvement and development.

❑ Affordability and housing development

Planning Policy Guidance Note 3 and DETR *Circular 13/96* set out key policy aspects:

- housing development schemes should generally incorporate a reasonable mix and balance of house types and sizes to cater for a range of needs;
- affordable housing is a material planning consideration; and
- targets for affordable housing should be set down in local plans.

Local authorities must be able to justify the targets which are set, and have defined what they mean by affordable. This requires local authority housing and planning departments to work together with public and private housing providers. In relation to housing and anti-poverty strategies, it is particularly important to consider the following issues:

- the scale of affordable housing provision;

- clear and justified guidance on what constitutes affordable housing;
- the relevance of low cost home ownership initiatives – will they provide a foot on the ladder of owner occupation? or will they create a further group of households on the margins of poverty? and
- the need to avoid large concentrations of new social housing provision on specific sites, especially peripheral urban locations.

Leicester City Council has researched affordability over four years, culminating in the publication in November 1996 of *Supplementary Planning Guidance on Affordable Housing*. This guidance includes information on:

- a review of affordability – using a report published in 1994 which indicated that over 65% of single households and more than 50% of households with two adults could not afford mortgage payments for full owner occupation (Brown, 1994);
- the shortfall of affordable housing – which currently stands at nearly 850 units per year;
- the mix and type of new social housing which is required – including priority for family housing;
- the location of new social housing provision; and
- confirmation of the local plan target – of at least 30% affordable housing being provided on sites of over 40 dwellings.

❑ Energy efficiency

Fuel costs form a major part of low income household budgets. While the average household expenditure on fuel and power in 1994/5 was 4.6% of total expenditure, the figure rose to 11% for those with the lowest 10% of incomes.

Fuel, like food, is often part of the budget which gets cut to meet unexpected costs. This results in both disconnections and arrears. The Child Poverty Action Group found in 1994 that 44,000 income support claimants had electricity deductions averaging £11.99 a week, while 185,000 claimants had gas deductions averaging £10.49 a week.

Compared to other European Union countries, such as Germany and the Netherlands, poor people in the UK suffer some of the worst problems in heating their homes. More than 1 in 10 households said that they could not afford to heat their homes adequately (Whyley et al, 1997), and 30% of UK households, about 20 million people, experience fuel poverty (*Poverty Matters*, 1993). This problem is aggravated both by the cold weather payments system, which requires seven consecutive days of cold weather before an additional payment is available under the UK welfare system, and by the poor standard of insulation in Britain's housing.

The benefits of tackling fuel poverty through energy efficiency initiatives are:

- more of the household budget can be spent on food and other necessities;
- improved health and comfort through steadier temperatures and reduced condensation and mould – which increase respiratory problems;
- fewer repair problems, fewer complaints, and less loss of rent due to prolonged voids turnaround;
- generation of local employment in respect of insulation programmes; and
- reduced emission of greenhouse gases, less depletion of finite resources, and a more sustainable environment.

The CIH has published a number of guides on this topic including a *Good Practice Briefing* on *Energy Efficiency* (CIH, 1996), and a *Directory of Energy Efficient Housing* (Lowe et al, 1996). In addition, the National Energy Agency has produced a series of guides on improving energy efficiency in the home including a study on improving energy awareness among ethnic minority households (NEA, 1997). All of these studies give an overview of the action individual landlords can take on insulation of older stock, design of new homes and replacement heating systems and energy advice to tenants.

Leicester City Council has been one of the lead authorities on energy efficiency, with a strong commitment to the environmental objectives of the Rio de Janeiro Summit, and was designated as Britain's first environmental city.

The Council surveyed public and private sector housing to identify the scale of investment needed to improve standards. Its strategy includes:

- training front line housing management staff to advise on energy issues;
- setting up an energy advice centre – which offers advice on home improvement grants, care and repair schemes as well as other energy saving initiatives; and
- issuing a loyalty card – which would give holders access to energy efficient goods, like saverplugs and low energy electrical products.

The individual initiatives are linked to the Council's overall strategic objective to reduce carbon dioxide emissions to half of the 1990 levels by 2025. Each activity is assessed for its contribution to the strategic target. The Housing Department has produced a Home Energy Conservation Act Report (1996b) which provides a strategic perspective for housing issues. It includes a ward profile, a review of energy strategies between 1990-96, and proposed measures and targets. The latter include, for example, financial advice for fuel poor households, energy advice, and a range of home energy efficiency packages.

Hastoe Housing Association operates in London and the Home Counties and owns 700 properties on 16 estates. In 1995 it reviewed its energy efficiency and affordable warmth policies. It now has a wide range of actions including:

- an Energy Advice Strategy – all tenants get energy advice and 20 members of staff now have a City & Guilds qualification in energy awareness;
- an Energy Advice Pack is provided to all new tenants in new properties;
- the appointment in 1997 of a maintenance supervisor to oversee the implementation of energy efficiency work in the existing stock; and
- the review of water conservation and wider environmental issues.

❑ Estate redevelopment

Urban regeneration and estate redevelopment has been a major element in tackling poverty and deprivation since the 1960s. Much of the emphasis for the last 10-15 years has been on physical redevelopment of, for example, hard-to-let estates by social landlords. In recent years, however, there has been a growing emphasis on partnership and community involvement (Taylor, 1995). The time scale requirements of capital programmes can make involving local residents more difficult. Moreover, programmes such as Estate Action reflected a single agency approach. Nevertheless, the successful examples of estate regeneration tend to demonstrate partnership and local involvement.

Barne Barton, Plymouth

Formerly owned by the Ministry of Defence this suffered from problems typical of a large difficult-to-let estate. It had very few local facilities; 65% of households were dependent on benefits; and there was a high young population, with nearly 20% of children under four years of age compared to 6% for Plymouth as a whole. In addition, the estate had become stigmatised and was seen as a dumping ground for vulnerable families.

A multi-agency project involving a range of organisations was set up in 1995. It involved the health authority, social services, education, the police, the Ministry of Defence, the local authority housing department and four housing associations (Sanctuary HA, William Sutton Trust, Sovereign HA and Devon and Cornwall HA). Housing-related actions included:

- community planning exercises with local people to identify priorities;
- environmental improvements;
- internal modernisation work; and
- conversion of properties to provide a wider range of house types.

In addition, the following initiatives have been taken by other members of the multi-agency partnership:

- development of a community centre;
- support for a local community action group;
- training schemes; and
- health promotion events.

London Borough of Hackney's Comprehensive Estates Initiative (CEI) was developed in the mid 1990s to refurbish Hackney's system-built estates. It aims to tackle a range of problems on five estates including physical conditions, social problems, economic decline and a poor environment. A comprehensive approach has been adopted so as to avoid the piecemeal approaches of the past. Emphasis has been placed on:

- training for tenants and staff;
- generic housing management; and
- greater tenant involvement.

A range of new policies and practices have been introduced including:

- tenant homesteading – prospective tenants are given choice and flexibility in the refurbishment of badly damaged void properties which they choose to move into, and a two month rent free period;
- menu improvements – tenants can choose a higher specification for refurbishment in return for higher rents; and
- tenant improvement options – tenants can select a package of refurbishment extras.

❑ Community involvement and development

This topic has been widely reported and there are several good practice guides. The importance of community involvement in the development of housing and anti-poverty strategies has already been stressed in a number of case studies (e.g. The Garths Estate in Sunderland in Chapter 1). Emphasis has also been given to ideas such as 'planning for real', and the community regeneration initiatives in Scotland especially Glasgow.

Many of the approaches outlined below are related to initiatives reported elsewhere in this chapter, such as credit unions, and employment and economic regeneration projects. Nevertheless, community development can also revolve around less tangible aspects such as campaigning, and the enhancement of social networks and social capital (see Appendices). It includes involvement through a tenants' association, residents' group or representation on the board of a registered social landlord or local authority committees.

There is a wide agreement that the effective and lasting regeneration of disadvantaged social housing estates can only be achieved in partnership with the residents (McArthur et al, 1996). But strong community organisations only develop through a long term process of community development which requires extensive resources and support. Many community involvement projects, however, focus almost entirely on implementation rather than strategy. This often results in the exclusion of local people from a decision making input on the strategic direction of regeneration.

Angell Town Community Project, Lambeth

This Project was set up in 1987 by tenants on the Angell Town Estate in Brixton led by Dora Boatemah. Its aim was to tackle the economic and physical decline of the estate, particularly multiple deprivation.

However, one of the first achievements of the Project in the late 1980s was to defeat a proposal from the Conservative Government to transfer compulsorily the estate to private sector control through a 'housing action trust'. Following a campaign by the tenants led by Dora Boatemah, they won the right to vote on the Government's proposals and opted to remain with the local authority.

Since then, Angell Town Community Project has undertaken a wide range of initiatives including:

- refurbishing over 200 unused garages into workshop spaces and shop units;
- establishing community businesses such as a bar/restaurant, a recording studio, a hairdressing salon, a laundrette and a corner shop;
- setting up a nursery, a centre for pensioners, a jobshop and a youth club;
- running access courses for unemployed people;
- managing a programme (assisted by Oxford Brookes University) in which 70 deck access flats were converted into 42 street level entry flats and maisonettes as a pilot programme, which secured £60m of Estate Action funding.

As Dora Boatemah explained at the Chartered Institute of Housing Annual Conference in 1997, regeneration must involve more than bricks and mortar – the local community must be centrally involved.

Examples of community development such as this emphasise the importance for housing organisations of working with local people. The proposal announced by the Housing Corporation in summer 1997 for registered social landlords to develop community action plans as part of 'housing plus' is a recognition of this requirement.

Community involvement and development is not just about short and medium term physical and economic regeneration of an estate. It is also about involving local people in running small projects such as day care facilities, community transport schemes and credit unions. It is often assumed that residents of so-called problem estates are apathetic and that community life has disintegrated. Yet there is plenty of evidence to suggest that this is not the case. The Community Development Foundation has estimated that there may be as many as two million participants involved in running local small-scale projects.

Family Action in Rogerfield and Easterhouse (FARE), Glasgow

This is a voluntary organisation managed and run by local people. It attempts to employ local residents (which has the added advantages of ensuring that wages are spent in the local area) in delivering a wide range of services which include:

- youth work including organising activities in local schools for more than 300 children;
- providing low cost holidays for families living in the area;
- running advice and support counselling for local people; and
- providing a community centre in a former hard-to-let tenement block (which is leased from Glasgow City Council's Housing department).

Nevertheless, as Holman (1997) points out, the achievements should not be over-stated. Some of the projects supported by FARE have had to close because of lack of finance. This is a common problem. There is thus an obvious need for a funding strategy to support those neighbourhood groups which are integral to promoting stable communities in deprived areas.

Guide to further reading

Housing development core activities

Benjamin A (1997): Social Exclusion – The Fightback Starts Here!: *Roof*, Nov/Dec pp 32-33

CIH (various): *Good Practice Briefing Notes*: Coventry, CIH

Lowe R et al (1996): *Directory of Energy Efficient Housing*: Coventry, CIH

CHAPTER 6

ANTI-POVERTY INITIATIVES AND THE COMMUNITY

This chapter examines a range of **non-core activities** which housing organisations could make part of a housing and anti-poverty strategy – namely:

- tackling crime and anti-social behaviour;
- education;
- employment;
- local exchange trading schemes (LETS);
- community shops and businesses
- training and housing opportunities;
- health;
- credit unions; and
- utilities and fuel poverty.

❑ Introduction

Many of the topics and case studies outlined in this Guide illustrate initiatives which indicate a drift among housing organisations away from simple concentration on traditional core functions. Indeed, the announcement in summer 1997 by the Focus Housing Group in Birmingham, that it was investigating the potential of changing from a housing association into a social investment agency is illustrative of the extent of this switch in emphasis among some housing organisations.

Focus Housing Group and Social Investment Agencies

Focus Housing Group defines Social Investment Agencies (SIAs) as those which provide social goods and services, usually in partnership with others, to communities which experience significant and multiple disadvantages and a lack of opportunity and empowerment. Focus is developing the SIA approach because of:

- declining subsidies for housing development;
- rent increases;
- inner city decline;
- growing levels of unemployment especially among young people;
- lack of community facilities and social infrastructure; and
- high levels of dependency – over 90% of Focus' tenants are on housing benefit.

The Group argues that core activities supplemented by housing plus initiatives are insufficient. If Focus becomes a SIA it plans to build on the experience of their Community Regeneration Unit which, over the last three years, has been involved in taking the lead on SRB schemes in Aston, and been a partner in the Castle Vale Housing Action Trust.

The Government's welfare to work strategy has also resulted in some housing organisations considering how they should become involved in wider activities – especially as 15% of the resources from the release of capital receipts is expected to be linked to environmental regeneration.

Involvement in non-core activities raises issues which must be addressed by housing organisations intending to participate in such activities:

- whether housing organisations have the skills and resources to participate in such ventures without losing sight of their core functions;
- legal constraints which may prevent organisations participating. Registered social landlords cannot develop along the lines of the community development corporations set up in the USA, which manage 150,000 homes as well as addressing issues such as education, job creation, preventative health measures and tackling crime and vandalism (Tickell, 1992);

- the need to engage in multi-agency partnerships to pursue these non-core functions; and
- the balance between non-core and core activities must be resolved in the strategic planning process (see Chapter 3).

❑ Tackling crime and anti-social behaviour

A frequent demand by tenants on social housing estates is for better security. Crime and anti-social behaviour is a key factor contributing to the creation of so-called problem estates. Areas with actual or perceived high crime rates often become stigmatised, and only households with little or no choice move in. They are usually on low incomes and are welfare dependent. Social landlords and local communities have to get involved in tackling crime and anti-social behaviour. There are organisations and working groups involved specifically in providing advice and guidance on improving safety and security on social housing estates. They include the Local Authority Working Group on Anti-Social Behaviour and the Safe Neighbourhoods Unit.

Dundee City Council has calculated that its Housing Department spends nearly £1.5m per year rectifying criminal damage. It therefore has developed a range of initiatives to tackle the issues including:

- security patrols in occupied and empty blocks of flats;
- concierge schemes with comprehensive CCTV;
- design changes to estates using the principles of defensible space;
- working alongside the police and the 'safer cities' programme to improve security and tackle crime;
- use of injunctions to curb anti-social behaviour; and
- distributing mobile phones to tenants suffering harassment and victimisation.

The effects of these measures are significant including:

- 60% reduction in the costs associated with vandalism where security patrols have been introduced; and
- significant reductions among tenants about the fear of crime and anti-social behaviour. On the Whitfield Estate, over 60% of tenants considered that their neighbourhood was safer after a comprehensive package of measures was implemented.

Sunderland Metropolitan District Council has been involved in working in partnership with the local police to improve the quality of life for people living on large peripheral estates such as Pennywell, which consists of over 2,500 units built in the early 1950s.

The estate has high levels of unemployment – with some neighbourhoods having a rate of over 50%. It also has exceptionally low rates of educational attainment – less than 10% of 15 year olds passed five or more GCSE exams at grades A to C in 1995 compared to a national figure of 45%. In relation to crime, houses in Pennywell are burgled on average every three years compared to a national figure of once every 40 years. Initiatives taken by the local authority include:

- liaison with local police;
- target hardening – increasing the physical security of properties;
- extra resources for housing management and policing; and
- use of introductory tenancies (under the Housing Act 1996).

In 1997, the Council and the police set up a 'safer estates task force' of over 20 officers, including tenancy enforcement officers and police officers. Within nine months, house burglaries and car thefts had been cut by 40%, and drug offences by 50%.

Local voluntary sector initiatives involving tenants have been developed during the 1990s including the Pennywell Breakout Scheme. This provides activities for children and their families during the summer – thus combating problems of boredom and anti-social behaviour among some young people. The number of incidents reported to the local police during holiday periods has fallen in Pennywell, at a time when it has increased in other parts of Sunderland.

❑ Education

The links between educational attainment and poverty are highlighted in previous chapters, the appendices, and in some of the cases studies set out in this chapter. Improving education reduces inequality. Local agencies working together can address and contribute to the efforts being made at national level. This contribution can be through a number of initiatives:

- pre-school learning – nursery facilities;

- after school and holiday – home work clubs; and
- post-school clubs and youth policies.

Each of these is aimed at a different target group with a core education objective, but with differing secondary objectives.

The value of pre-school learning and constructive play has been stressed by many researchers (Edwards, 1992). Poor living conditions and lack of play space impact on child development. These effects can be mitigated by, for instance, pre-school activities and stimulating opportunities for social contact through a safe and interesting environment to play in (Wheway and Millward, 1997). Such projects may provide additional benefits. If the pre-school provision is provided at affordable prices or free, it can assist with child care for parents wishing to return to the labour market. It can also provide a welcome break for a parent during the week, allowing time for other activities.

The **Sunflower Nursery, Cambridge** provides 33 places for children aged 4 months to 5 years, and is part of a larger project providing housing and training. The nursery is open between 8.30 – 5.30 Monday to Friday, with parents able to choose between a 2, 3 or 5 day provision. The long opening hours give parents returning to work flexibility, and has added to the take up of places.

The scheme was developed by Cambridge Housing Society, with support from the Housing Corporation, which funded the building. The revenue costs, primarily staff and food, are meet from fees. The nursery has been investigating bursaries and aims to set up a fund – the interest from which will be used to finance up to half of the places.

The project includes a parents' room, where staff and parents can meet to discuss a child's development, and where the health visitor can hold a weekly clinic.

The management of the nursery is through a support group which contains members from Cambridge Housing Society, staff, parents and health and education professionals. The management committee has written terms of reference, which include personnel, monitoring standards and bursary funding.

The second aspect concerns after school and holidays. For middle class children, undertaking homework in their own room after returning from school enables assignments to be completed, often with the help of a computer and/or a supportive parent.

For low income households performance may be affected by overcrowding, lack of facilities, and damp or cold rooms. Homework clubs, which have proved popular on USA social housing estates (Tickell, 1992), offer an opportunity for supported study. They may also provide advice, counselling services and employment training. From the landlord's viewpoint, they keep children off the estate, where their play may cause nuisance or increase vandalism.

There are currently about 3,500 after-school/homework clubs catering for 150,000 five-twelve year olds. Funding is piecemeal, and includes the Government's out-of-school initiative, local authorities, charities and voluntary support. In November 1997, the Government announced a five year programme of out-of-school and homework clubs, costing £300 million. Over the period it is expected to provide up to a million places, and support homework clubs at half of all secondary schools and a quarter of all primary schools. It is important that these schemes build on existing projects represented by the Kids' Club Network, as well as schemes organised and supported by housing organisations.

The **Streetwise Project** is managed by Broomleigh Housing Association, Youth Action 2000, Bromley Education Department and Ravensbourne NHS Trust. It provides facilities for 10-18 year olds in the Penge and Anerley neighbourhoods.

Broomleigh Housing Association is a stock transfer association, and hence the major local landlord, with a high concentration of young people playing on its estates. It assisted with the development of a new facility, as Streetwise's existing premises were near the end of their lease. The new facility provides a mix of accommodation for young people and drop in advice, counselling and support. The revenue costs are met through grants to Youth Action 2000 which leases part of the building and provides the advice services.

❑ Employment

Housing organisations are becoming involved in a wide range of initiatives in this area including Local Exchange Trading Systems (LETS), local labour and training schemes, shops, and training and housing projects (including Foyers – see Chapter 2). There are considerable overlaps between employment initiatives, urban regeneration and estate refurbishment, community involvement and training schemes – the latter are dealt with later in this chapter.

There is a growing degree of commitment among housing organisations to housing and employment initiatives as a means of tackling poverty. Holmes (as quoted in Taylor, 1995) comments in a study of housing and community regeneration that:

> *"The change that would most improve life is the prospect of full employment and bringing a full wage packet home".*

Physical regeneration involves the spending of many millions of pounds with potential benefits for the local economy in terms of investment and jobs – the multiplier effect. Investment in housing, especially modernisation and repairs, is labour intensive and can have an immediate impact on local economies. Employment and training initiatives can respond to customer orientated approaches and community needs – e.g. affordable warmth initiatives (see McGregor et al, 1995).

Nevertheless, there are dangers with an over-optimistic stance, including:

- research on inner city initiatives in British and American cities over the last 30-40 years suggests that it is not easy to ensure that newly created jobs and training opportunities go to local people;
- large flagship schemes do not create jobs for those at the bottom end of the labour market, as the filtering down of opportunities is an extremely slow process;
- jobs and training opportunities created for local people may often be low paid, short term or part time;
- the type of jobs created may not match local potential or future needs;
- the training requirement may be inappropriate – John Watson, the former Chief Executive of Bradford City Challenge pointed out at the CIH Annual Conference in 1997 that construction companies involved in the regeneration of the Homewood Estate were obliged to offer training opportunities to local people, yet many of the 25% unemployed local people were already builders or joiners; and

- relatively few attempts have been made to encourage service-based employment – the idea of 'resident services organisations' which would employ local people to provide intensive levels of services is, as Saunders (1997) suggests, an intriguing possibility worth exploring.

Nevertheless, there are many types of initiative being pursued by housing organisations in conjunction with other bodies. Many of these schemes originated in the pioneering work by local authorities in the late 1970s and 1980s on local economic development strategies.

In **Sheffield** there have been local employment projects on the Manor Estate since the early 1980s (Dean, 1995). These have been developed by the local community and by Sheffield City Council's Employment and Economic Development Division. By the early 1990s, a training and resource centre had been developed and workshop units were being constructed using local labour. The principles behind these schemes included community control of strategic decisions, using local labour, and capacity building for local people. Nevertheless, unemployment in the mid 1990s was about 25% which was double the average for Sheffield.

This example clearly illustrates the difficulties of achieving a significant impact through local projects as well as reminding housing organisations that they need to work with other organisations and local communities.

❑ Local Exchange Trading Systems (LETS)

LETS are local non-profit exchange networks in which all kinds of goods and services can be traded without the need for money. The system uses a local notional currency, which enables members to exchange goods and services. The roots of LETS can be traced back to the 19th Century co-operative movement in Europe and the USA, barter currencies in the 1930s, and the UK skills exchange networks and business barter clubs in the 1970s. LETS schemes have spread across Europe, the Americas and have grown most rapidly in the UK.

The UK developed its own model of LETS from 1990 onwards. Since then over 400 LETS have been established – typically with a few hundred members. Appendix 5 is a set of rules for a LETS devised by LETSlink UK.

The principle behind LETS is self help, mutual aid and equality of opportunity. Members get credits for work they do, which they have to spend within the scheme. It encourages local trade, and keeps the wealth generated available locally – unlike conventional money, which with globalisation, follows the highest return. As a system, which instead relies on labour, not cash, each member has an equal ability to issue currency.

The formation of a LETS club is simpler than many other initiatives. It requires a group of members, who pay a fee to cover running costs – which will be low if administration is done by volunteers. Members receive a personal account book, a cheque book and details of other members and the services they are offering. Members buy a service at a negotiated price from another member, for which they write a cheque. The transaction is recorded, when the cheque is passed to the administrator, so each member's account of spending is kept up to date.

Successful LETS schemes in **Manchester**, **Reading** and **West Wiltshire** reveal the following requirements:

- **a wide range of skills** – the scheme should not be dominated by one group or trade. It needs child minders, but also car repairers, painters, gardeners, plumbers and car drivers;
- **good up-to-date information** – on who is offering which service. This requires the voluntary committee or administrator to produce a regular quarterly newsletter;
- **flexibility** – so that cash can be mixed with the local currency to allow for materials. This may be necessary where someone is offering to drive people say to the airport. The driver's time would be paid in LETS currency and the fuel costs in cash; and
- **a limit for maximum debt.** People inevitably go into debt to start the process. In at least one case a member ran up large LETS debts without putting services or goods back into the system. The debt limit needs to be agreed by members and reflect the size of the scheme.

LETS are a grey area for tax and benefits, but most experience to date is positive. LETS income is usually viewed as payment in kind for benefit purposes, as it is a small scale activity – so as long as the claimant remains available for work and contributes less than 16 hours a week. For businesses which participate in the system, the situation is less clear. If the sum of the activities remains small, they tend to be treated by the Inland Revenue as favours to friends. However, if the activity forms part of their overall trade, they will be liable for tax.

❑ Local labour schemes

Local authorities and housing associations have encouraged local labour initiatives over the past decade, but much of this work has been unsuccessful or short term. Authorities are constrained by the Local Government Act 1988, which treats local labour contracts as unfair competition. Some have developed on-going relationships with specific contractors, and negotiated local labour and training opportunities outside of the construction contract. These initiatives have not always been successful. But they demonstrate that housing organisations need to understand the specific features of the local labour market, including the attitudes and perceptions of contractors (McGregor et al, 1995).

Local labour schemes are primarily linked to construction activity or responsive repairs contracts. The aim is to target employment opportunities, which come from capital investment, towards the local labour market, thus securing a double gain for the community of new or improved homes and new skills and employment. Outside contractors may also sub-contract work to smaller local firms.

Elements which increase the prospects of success have been identified by People for Action (1996). These are:

- **corporate commitment** – with development and technical staff understanding the strategy and how the employment initiatives can help stimulate employment opportunities;
- **documentation** – needs to explicitly state the requirements for local labour and how this must be fulfilled by the main contractor, e.g. through a percentage of person days being let to local sub-contractors, or a percentage of person days using local labour;
- **monitoring** – using methods agreed before the contract is entered into. This is likely to include regular reports submitted by the contractor to the client and monthly review;

- **selection** – of local labour should be the responsibility of the contractor. The client may provide a pool of possible employees or a list of possible sub-contractors from which the main contractor selects; and
- **provisional sums** – to cover additional costs if the contractor is required to appoint low productivity staff, or those with training or other needs.

The experience of recent schemes has been more successful, particularly during the recession in the building industry, because the balance of power in negotiating contracts has marginally shifted towards the clients. Housing associations using local labour schemes have been setting targets of 25-40% in respect of local labour. This works out at about 1,500-2,400 person days on a £1 million construction contract. However, with the recent upturn in the building industry, it is difficult to predict whether this success will continue.

The Government are reviewing the legislation which forces local authorities to ignore non-commercial considerations when placing contracts. The Chartered Institute of Housing has argued strongly the merits of being able to use capital and revenue spending so as to help regenerate local communities through employment.

Oldham MBC and South East Lancashire Housing Association

The housing association is a community based association, managing rented housing predominantly in Lancashire. It manages a 450 unit deck access block in Primrose Bank in Oldham, on behalf of the Council.

The estate has a high level of benefit dependency, and employment generation was made part of the Estate Action programme. This was achieved through clauses in the works contract which required that 10% local labour be employed – drawn from a skills pool made up from referrals and Employment Service records.

While there were initial difficulties in securing contractor compliance with the local labour objective, due to poor drafting of the contact, the clause was tightened in later phases of the work.

Shokoya Eleshin Construction Ltd is a private construction company which combines urban regeneration with jobs for local people. It was set up in 1992 to compete for building contracts and at the same time to employ local people, especially from ethnic minorities. As the company lacked a track record, it had to develop links with local housing associations and large construction companies.

It has now been successfully involved in schemes in Blackburn and Liverpool. In the latter, it has worked in partnership with Steve Biko Housing Association and Alfred McAlpine on an inner city housing development scheme of 41 new properties. Over 60 jobs were created and 50% of these have gone to people from the immediate vicinity and 75% to people living in the broad Liverpool conurbation. In Blackburn, the company worked with North British Housing Association and Alfred McAlpine on a project to provide 13 four bedroom properties. The company was able to use nearly 75% local labour of which over 20% was from ethnic minorities.

❑ Community shops and businesses

This is a difficult subject. There are numerous examples of past failures. Unlike local labour initiatives that may fail to employ local labour, the failure of a shop causes both job redundancy and financial loss to the sponsoring organisation. The risks need to be properly analysed at the start, by considering:

- what is the project trying to achieve?
- how does the shop, rather than another initiative, meet the objective?
- is there demand for the services, and at what level for what price?
- what level of subsidy will the organisation provide, for how long?
- what criteria will it use to assess success or failure?

The objective in establishing a community shop may be to provide local people with access to products or a service not available on the estate or in the neighbourhood. This may be a launderette or a fresh fruit and vegetable shop. The shop may also provide employment, training in dealing with people and money, and aid community development.

There are likely to be good commercial reasons why retailers have decided not to locate in the area. This may be due to lack of trade or to social problems. If shopping facilities are needed, it may be better to attract an existing retailer to the area with a subsidy such as a rent free period. If the trade will not materialise, there may be more effective alternative employment or training options.

As well as community involvement, the market must be researched to find out if there is not only a need, but also a demand for the goods and services that the proposed shops will provide. Evidence is required that local people will be willing to use the facility on a frequent basis, and that they are willing to pay the appropriate prices for goods and services.

In addition to concerns about lack of demand, a community shop may face problems of a lack of skills and a need for long term subsidy. Shop management is an underrated skill, but requires forward planning, estimating demand for products, financial and staff management. These are valuable skills to develop, but may be lacking. The subsidy too requires consideration. It may be from the landlord as a rent free period, or a reduced rent for the full term. Or, it could be given as sponsorship, providing direct support to the business – covering start up costs or working capital or subsidising trading losses.

The Boundary Estate Launderette, Tower Hamlets

The project came out of tenant frustration at the lack of a local launderette, and the lack of individual laundry facilities due to low incomes. It was proposed in 1988, and for four years the tenants' group carried out market research, and pursued funding and premises. Support comes from East London Partnership, a business lead organisation, City Action, the Church Urban Fund and the London Borough of Tower Hamlets, which has provided the premises at an affordable rent.

The project employs three local people (including two Bengali speakers because Bengali people are the largest minority ethnic group in the area). The business is run by a board of tenant directors and any surpluses are ploughed back into the estate's tenants' association.

The success of the project has stimulated confidence on the estate to consider other community initiatives including an associated ironing business, and a second hand clothes business, using the laundry to clean donated items.

Community businesses and the Angell Town Community Project, Lambeth

The Angell Town Community Project has been described earlier. A vital aspect of the Project's work is linking community regeneration with local employment initiatives, partly through helping to establish community businesses. The Project has encouraged the establishment of community businesses such as a bar/restaurant, a recording studio, a hairdressing salon, a launderette and a 'corner shop'.

Angell Town Community Project has learned that the success of a community business approach requires:

- overcoming apathy and stigma so that business success breeds self-confidence among local residents;
- commitment and support of the local community;
- realistic assessment of the demand for the goods and services produced by potential community businesses;
- overcoming external constraints including challenging the scepticism of private funders and the local authority; and
- training support for developing and running community businesses.

Even so, some community businesses in Angell Town have failed. The reasons for this include lack of business skills, too much reliance on volunteers, and lack of business support. Nevertheless, the Project shows that with community support especially from young people, these types of businesses can help local regeneration.

❑ Training and housing opportunities

The three case studies in this section illustrate the links between training, housing and employment. In the case of the self-build projects, the schemes increase and enhance the participants' confidence and self-esteem, with potential benefits for many aspects of their lives, and their activity within society.

Community self-build

The Sound Image Self-Build Project in the London Borough of Brent provides move-on accommodation for homeless young people together with National Vocational Qualification training. Despite slow recruitment, 12 young people did move into homes they helped to build. And, they all achieved the relevant NVQ (Hart and McGettigan, 1997).

The Wise Group is a series of not-for-profit businesses, developed in Glasgow in the mid 1980s. During the mid 1990s, the Group has expanded its activities to locations such as Derby and Newham as well as rural areas in Scotland. By the end of 1995, the Group employed nearly 250 people and had 600 trainees.

The Group activities are – first, Heatwise which provides products and services including home insulation, heating systems and home security; second, Landwise which does environmental improvements. The Group improves housing and living conditions, and substantially benefits household incomes by reducing fuel bills. McGregor et al (1997) confirm that independent assessment of the quality of work undertaken by the Group has been extremely positive.

The Wise Group is committed to carrying out regeneration schemes by recruiting, training and managing a workforce drawn from long term unemployed people. Each trainee has an eight week induction period followed by a 44 week work contract. During the period of their work contract, participants are paid the rate for the job which is currently around £120 per week. The scheme thus provides more than basic training, and participants gain a NVQ. Economists regard this initiative as part of the intermediate labour market.

The scheme has helped long term unemployed people in Glasgow back into the full labour market. About 65% of participants had found a job at some point after leaving the scheme. Nearly 50% were still in employment 6 months after leaving the scheme. This compares with only 25% who were on the Government's training for work programme in Glasgow.

The success of the Wise Group has been achieved through the support of local authorities, such as Glasgow City Council, who are the main buyers of the products and services.

East Northamptonshire District Council – Rushden Renovate

This project tackles youth unemployment, social problems and housing needs in East Northants District Council (ENDC) particularly among disaffected young people:

- with learning difficulties;
- leaving care; and
- leaving youth custody;
- who could not access standard training packages, and who need counselling and support. It addresses social exclusion as well as dealing with unemployment and low incomes.

ENDC and Northamptonshire CC Social Services were aware that the needs of disaffected young people were not being met. Analysis of the waiting list showed an increasing demand for social housing by young people. **Rushden Renovate** is part of a wider package of measures for young people including, from a housing viewpoint – a rent deposit scheme, access to social housing, and move-on accommodation. From a training perspective, opportunities exist to access college courses. On-going support for young people from Social Services is available from the Youth Service Section.

The project gives advice, counselling and support by a qualified youth/social worker, and provides 14 one bedroom self-contained flats in a converted shoe factory in Rushden – one unit will be fully accessible for a disabled person.

Training in construction, health and safety, and basic numeracy and communication is provided so as to improve employability. Training is provided on the rehabilitation site and four of the trainees will be offered accommodation in the completed scheme. However, access to advice and support is not dependant on participating in the training programme.

During the course of the Project young people were provided, if necessary, with supported accommodation in a nearby scheme managed by English Churches Housing Group. Others were provided with transport to the project.

Referrals come from many sources including Careers Offices, Social Services, Head Teachers and the Probation Service as well as self-referral. East Northamptonshire is a large and diverse area and in order for the project to cater for the needs of disaffected young people throughout the district, a minibus is used to transport them into the training and advice project.

The project is a partnership between:

- **East Northants District Council** – who organise and co-ordinate the overall programme, and have 100% nomination rights. The council successfully bid for DoE housing partnership funding of £139,500, and are using £139,500 Local Authority Social Housing Grant;
- **Northamptonshire CC Social Services** – which provides over £20,000 a year for full time social/youth worker, and is a referral point for disaffected young people;
- **Touchstone Housing Association** – which levered in £297,870 of private finance as well as gaining support of the Housing Corporation; and
- **Northamptonshire Chamber of Commerce TEC**: which provides training places in construction/numeracy/communication skills to NVQ standard for 10 young people. Funding of £49,000 from EU Social Fund which has paid, for example, for the minibus.

❑ Health

Ill health is frequently a product of social conditions, and there is a clear link between health, housing and inequality. The Government is strongly committed to tackling these links. The Minister for Public Health, Tessa Jowell, highlighted in July 1997 that 'government policies for a minimum wage, welfare to work, improved housing, and education would have a marked effect on people's health'. Local authorities and other housing providers can, therefore, address health issues through their anti-poverty work and inter-agency links.

Local Health Authorities are required to produce an annual report on public health. A number of these organisations have focused attention on poor health, bad housing and low incomes. Sheffield Health Authority in its 1994 Annual Report emphasised the issue of housing and homelessness. The authority identified twice as many attendances at hospital accident and emergency departments from deprived electoral wards compared with better off wards.

A partnership strategy is needed which is community centred and involves many organisations. A number of UK cities have been involved in the World Health Organisation Healthy Cities Project set up in 1986. The project promotes innovation and change in local health policy. There are four designated cities in Britain – Liverpool, Camden in London, Glasgow and Belfast. They are exploring ways to translate the principles of the European Health for All strategy into practice. Other cities across the UK are also pursuing the Health for All agenda including Sheffield, Birmingham, Kirklees, Norwich and Londonderry (Laughlin and Black, 1995).

Sheffield Health 2000

Sheffield has committed itself to reducing inequalities in health within the city as a long term objective. The Healthy Sheffield partnership consists of a local authority and the health authority working with eight other partner organisations representing voluntary and community groups.

The partnership's Health for All strategy is based on extensive consultation with local people and organisations and has identified 17 priority issues for health and specific objectives for action. The process also identified three central themes – poverty, discrimination and the environment. The Our City – Our Health Framework for Action co-ordinates the development of specific strategies, and a detailed action planning process, which outlines actions and responsibilities within the partnership.

Delivering a vision of Health for All in Sheffield involves key ways of working, which the partnership is committed to:

- **community development** – action needs to take place locally and to involve local people. Supporting active participation is crucial and the initiative provides small grants, training and infrastructure support for development and health;

- **organisational development** – this involves working within organisations to create effective structures and policies, and become open, flexible and accountable, and encourage participation. Training, information and support for corporate policy development are among the tools used by the partnership;
- **education and training** – the partnership has provided training for many groups from health visitors to community sector groups; and
- **information sharing** – between organisations is vital. This helps to reduce overlaps and increases integration.

Linked to this was an expressed need for improved planning, to fill gaps in health service provision, and make best use of resources. The next step in Sheffield's programme is to work up a series of specific initiatives within the strategic framework.

❑ Credit unions

Credit unions are savings and loan groups where members can save at a level to suit themselves and borrow at a reasonable rate of interest. Each union is owned and controlled by its members.

Credit unions can trace their roots back to 1849 in Germany. They have spread world wide, with high levels of membership in Canada and USA. It is estimated that 95 million people world wide belong to one of the 71,000 credit unions in operation. The development of credit unions in the UK has been slower, although with the support of the National Consumer Council the movement is beginning to take off, with groups such as the London Taxi Drivers forming a credit union which has assets of over £1 million (ABCUL, 1993).

The philosophy behind credit unions is that people can achieve far more by working together, than by individual effort. They promote community welfare and stimulate learning opportunities for the voluntary members who run them. They offer a facility for regular savings, and loans at a reasonable rate of interest.

In areas without banking facilities or where minimum deposits apply, credit unions offer banking facilities to the 19% of the population who do not have a bank account (*Poverty Matters*, 1993). In Birmingham, nearly 30% of the population has no local access to banking services, or is on the verge of losing it.

There are over 550 credit unions in Britain. Membership has grown from 88,000 in 1992 to 161,000 in 1995. Despite this, credit unions remain relatively small. Ladywood Community Credit Union in Birmingham has only 270 members and savings of £55,000. Workplace based credit unions are often small scale but, with trade union support, have been growing.

Credit unions are regulated by the Registry of Friendly Societies and by the Credit Union Act 1979. Membership of a credit union is restricted to those with a common bond. The principle is that the common bond increases concern, loyalty and trust. The common bond may be generated in three ways:

- an **occupational bond** – such as a credit union for employees; or
- an **associational bond** – like the taxi drivers; or
- a **community bond** – for those living in a certain area.

Membership is gained by starting a personal savings plan. This may be a small but regular amount. Savings attract interest, although the rates are usually lower than building society accounts. Savings also attract insurance, so if a member dies their next of kin will receive a payment in proportion to their savings.

The main attraction for members is cheap loans. For low income households, commercial loans are frequently not available, or only at high interest rates. Credit unions are able to lend at low rates in comparison to commercial unsecured loans, usually at 1% per month (APR 12.7%).

The credit union is run in a similar way to most co-operative organisations, through a voluntary board elected by members at an annual general meeting, with accounts available to members.

There has been growing interest in credit unions and a number of housing associations, like Enterprise 5 Housing Association, have pioneered their development in the association sector. In the case of Enterprise 5 Housing Association, the credit union is run outside of the association by a tenants' federation, but with membership available to both employees and tenants. In order to promote further the role of credit unions among housing associations, People for Action 2001 have been funded by the Housing Corporation to help set them up. In local government a number of authorities, including Liverpool, Newcastle and Sheffield, have units to stimulate the growth of credit unions.

Sheffield Credit Union Development Agency (SCUDA) was set up in 1990 with funding from the City Council, as part of its anti-poverty strategy. Initial funding was for two development workers and an administration worker.

The management of the agency is through the credit unions which it has established and which it continues to support. It is independently registered as a company limited by guarantee, with a board elected by its members.

Its primary function has been working within inner city Sheffield to stimulate credit unions, primarily with a community common bond. SCUDA has, however, extended its activities beyond the inner area and stimulated a number of employee/associational schemes.

During the first five years the Agency has generated 11 credit unions. Nine of them are community based, and they cover a third of the area of Sheffield. The average membership is small, about 150. This has lead to two unions negotiating a merger to reduce costs and thus increase benefits for members. This is likely to be a growing trend, with neighbouring housing estate credit unions coming together. In the USA and Canada unions have an average of 3-4,000 members, compared with 1,000 in Britain and Ireland.

Of the employee based credit unions, the most successful is based around Mainline Buses. During its first year of operation it generated over 500 members and is continuing to grow.

The Sheffield experience suggests a continued interest in community based unions, as word of mouth spreads the success story. The key to success is balancing a close knit community bond with a large enough area to make the credit union viable.

More rapid growth, however, is likely to come through employee based credit unions, following the success of Mainline, as employers see such schemes as a benefit in attracting and retaining staff which has no direct cost to the company.

To date, credit union development has been largely restricted to urban areas (Thomas and Balloch, 1994). The National Consumer Council, which played a key role in establishing the legal framework and promoting credit unions, is now keen to see them extend into rural areas. The need in rural Britain is likely to be as strong, with the decline in rural post offices, lack of banking facilities and high levels of low paid employment (Wales Co-operative Centre, 1995). A project supported by the Rural Development Commission and Joseph Rowntree Foundation successfully developed two credit unions in the Pennines. The project found that the urban credit union model does not always transplant into rural areas, as account must be taken of local issues. However, the success of credit unions in rural Ireland suggests there is unfulfilled potential.

❑ Utilities and fuel poverty

An anti-poverty strategy requires landlords to work with other agencies. One set of key agencies is the utilities, who supply fuel and water, and whose charging policies can have dramatic effects on low income household.

For all utilities, disconnection policies have toughened since privatisation. An independent agency can ensure policies are operated sensitively, and can save individual disconnections. In the case of water companies, disconnection can be a major problem for housing association tenants in newer accommodation where metering has been installed (Passmore, 1995). Evidence suggests that water metering for the average family increases water costs, with low average households spending 4% of their weekly income on water compared to 1% for the national average (Cunninghame et al, 1995). The effect on low income households is to push people into arrears.

Social Services Departments have a stop power contained in each company's licence – condition H7 (3) (1). This gives Social Services power to require deferment of disconnection indefinitely and unconditionally. There has been recent moves by water companies to introduce pre-payment systems. Some authorities are concerned that such arrangements effectively cause self-disconnection.

Gas and electric utilities have been pursuing similar pre-payment policies. This has enabled utilities to reduce their disconnection statistics. However, growing numbers of low income households have periods of the week or fortnight without using fuel – again, effectively self-disconnection (Fitch, 1995). Pre-payment is also more expensive. For gas, pre-payment costs about 12% more than quarterly bills.

Local agencies working together can encourage utilities to review their practices. However, more effective action can be achieved through the regulator – OFWAT, OFGAS and OFTEL. Local authority associations could ensure that standards be monitored more effectively, by negotiating with the regulators on codes of practice on disconnection, pre-payments and low income users.

Guide to further reading

Non-core activities

Brown T and Passmore J (1996): *Poverty and Social Housing*: Sevenoaks, Moat Housing Group

Chartered Institute of Housing (1995): *A Point to Prove*: Coventry, CIH

Dwelly T (Ed) (1996): *Living in the Future – 24 Sustainable Development Ideas From the UK*: Coventry, Habitat International

The Housing Corporation (1997): *A Housing Plus Approach to Achieving Sustainable Communities*: London, The Housing Corporation

New Economics Foundation (undated): *Community Works – A Guide to Community Economic Action*: London, NEF

Power A with Richardson L (1996): *Housing Plus – An Agenda for Social Landlords?*: London, London School of Economics

Taylor M (1995): *Unleashing the Potential – Bringing Residents to the Centre of Regeneration*: York, Joseph Rowntree Foundation

CHAPTER 7

RESOURCES

This chapter:

- considers the funding and resourcing issues associated with implementing a strategy; and
- draws attention to the significance of monitoring and evaluation.

❑ Resources

Discussions of resource availability usually refer primarily to funding. However, the term has a wider meaning which encompasses, for instance, legal resources (e.g. what statutory limitations and opportunities are there for implementing policies?). It also includes human resources – the skills and expertise of the individual participants who will be implementing elements of the anti-poverty strategies.

■ Legal resources

There is no direct general legal requirement for social housing organisations to engage in anti-poverty activities, although some voluntary housing trusts may be required to do so by their founding deed. However, there are many regulations which **encourage** social housing organisations to reflect poverty and social exclusion considerations. Organisations which only work to the minimum legal requirements will fail to develop innovative policies and practices.

Nevertheless, there are legal restrictions on what housing organisations can do. This is illustrated by the decision of the Focus Housing Group in

Birmingham to seek registration with the Charity Commissioners as a social investment agency to change its current status as a housing association. This will allow Focus to extend the scope of its activities, for example, into community safety, transport, community care and play facilities.

Performance standards and the tenants guarantee for registered social landlords in England and their equivalents in Scotland and Wales are also focused narrowly on housing. Housing and anti-poverty initiatives, as well as housing plus, would be strongly aided if they explicitly encouraged the adoption of a broader based approach – leading possibly to the community development corporation model of the USA or the community development trust and social investment agency concept currently being developed in the UK.

There are thus both limitations and grey areas as to what registered social landlords can currently do. Their constitutional objects must be within the limitations set by statute. Moreover, capital grants cannot be used for non-housing purposes. But each organisation is expected to decide for itself whether it is operating within these constraints. Regulators' guidance on what constitutes 'housing purposes' would bring certainty, but would also bring restrictions. Many registered social landlords thus prefer to be left to themselves to decide the legitimate parameters of their operations.

Local authorities have a wide range of legislative requirements which enable them to adopt a more proactive approach. There is no statutory requirement for local government to prepare housing and anti-poverty strategies. However, the Local Government and Housing Act 1989, for example, requires local authorities to prepare an annual economic development plan if they wish to spend resources on this topic – clearly aspects of housing and anti-poverty strategies could be included. In addition, the Home Energy and Conservation Act 1995 requires affected local authorities to produce a strategy which could be used as part of an input into an anti-poverty policy.

■ Human resources

The skills of staff working in housing organisations affect the successful implementation of anti-poverty initiatives. The philosophy underpinning housing and anti-poverty strategies is that housing organisations **must** extend their horizons. Innovative ways of acting and thinking are required.

This innovation is, at least in part, likely to come from staff. The often quoted phrase, 'staff are the organisation's most valuable asset', is as relevant for housing and anti-poverty activities as it is for other tasks. The key questions are:

- have the staff the necessary inter-disciplinary and transferable skills to work in this new environment; and
- how can the necessary skills be developed and promoted?

Current training programmes do not adequately address this need.

■ Financial resources

Many anti-poverty strategies highlight the range of competitive bidding schemes which could be used to finance activities. Wakefield Metropolitan District Council's Anti-Poverty Strategy states that it will make representations and bids for funding from the following sources:

- Challenge Funding;
- Church Urban Fund;
- European Regional Development Fund;
- European Social Fund;
- Housing Corporation;
- Housing Partnership;
- Lottery Funding;
- Millennium Funds; and
- Single Regeneration Bid.

To this list could be added a number of other potential competitive bidding schemes which have been, or are being, used such as Rural Challenge, City Challenge, Estate Renewal Challenge Funding, and resources from the Government's capital receipts initiative. In addition, other sources might possibly be tapped including Housing Corporation Innovation and Good Practice Grants, and research funding from bodies such as the Joseph Rowntree Foundation.

The following three examples illustrate potential sources of external funding for anti-poverty activities.

Scotland and European Union Funding

Although housing is not a European Union (EU) competence, anti-poverty initiatives form an element of EU regional and social policy. An unpublished report for Scottish Homes by Chapman et al (1994) indicates that Scotland has made considerable use of EU funding for housing-related projects, many of which also address anti-poverty issues.

Schemes mentioned in the report include:

- the use of £2.6m European Social Fund money per year by the **Wise Group** (see Chapter 6) for training purposes and labour costs;
- the **Pilton Poverty Group** in Edinburgh which drew in over £2m from the EU to create a community development strategy to address social and welfare issues. The expertise of staff in the District and Regional Councils played a significant part in helping the Group to obtain this funding; and
- EU funding amounting to 4.7m ecus was obtained for an innovative community development project for the **Ferguslie Park** area of Paisley which consists in part of a large problem estate. Again, the expertise of staff working in the Ferguslie Park Partnership was vital in obtaining these funds.

Partick Housing Association, Clydeside

This housing association obtained £0.4m from the European Regional Development Fund Community Initiatives scheme in the mid 1990s, to renovate a multi-storey vacant building into 13 flats and 15 workshop units (Stephens et al, 1996). The Community Initiatives scheme aims to help to tackle poverty, social exclusion and unemployment through infrastructure and business investments. The European Union input was matched by funding from other sources including private loans, Glasgow Development Agency and Scottish Homes.

Initially, the association had obtained a guarantee of funds from these other agencies for the upper storey conversion, but could not get resources for the ground floor refurbishment. Strathclyde European Partnership, which provided help and advice on European funding mechanisms, worked with Partick Housing Association to gain access to the Community Initiatives fund.

Leicester Newark Housing Association and National Lottery Charities Board Funding

Leicester Newark Housing Association manages nearly 400 units of furnished accommodation for young people and students on low incomes in inner Leicester.

In 1994, it became increasingly concerned about the poor condition of two of its large shared properties. The local authority and the Housing Corporation did not prioritise the proposed modernisation scheme. As a last resort, the association sought grant aid from the National Lottery Charities Board under the theme of assisting young people on low incomes.

This bid was successful in October 1995 and the association received £160,000 towards the total refurbishment costs of over £270,000. Twelve self-contained furnished flats are being provided at a rent of £36 per week – excluding common area service charges. This is about £15 per week lower than similar accommodation in the private rented sector and thus helps young people secure affordable accommodation.

Aston Reinvestment Trust: A Social Investment Fund for Birmingham

The Trust was established in 1997 to help finance urban regeneration, create jobs and provide new opportunities for the inner areas of Birmingham. It lends money at commercial rates to businesses, community development schemes and voluntary sector projects which find it difficult to access conventional funding – because of a lack of an asset base and/or a track record. It draws its inspiration from schemes in the USA such as the South Shore Bank of Chicago which has been undertaking similar work for nearly 25 years.

The aim is to attract £0.5m from individual investors and institutions in the first year of operation and to secure a £3.5m loan fund by 2000. The board members of the Trust are drawn from the public and private sectors and include people with considerable business expertise. The Trust also works closely with other organisations including Birmingham City Pride, Birmingham City Council, Birmingham Settlement and the local Training and Enterprise Council.

The Trust makes loans in the following areas:

- small and medium size businesses;
- voluntary organisations and charities;
- affordable housing – including a property loans service targeted at housing co-operatives, self-build projects, and community-based and minority ethnic housing associations; and
- energy saving schemes.

However, there are pitfalls with **relying** on external competitive sources, including:

- **abortive work** on schemes which fail to win approval;
- the **limited scale** of funding which is available through these initiatives and competitions;
- **uncertain criteria** which housing and anti-poverty initiatives may not meet for some of these competitive bidding schemes. Thus the amount of leakage into housing and anti-poverty initiatives may well be extremely small scale; and
- the **time and resources** involved for housing organisations to identify and work with partners skilled in obtaining external funding.

This suggests that housing and anti-poverty strategies need to look elsewhere for funding sources. **Redirecting internal financial resources**, and the top-slicing of existing budgets for prioritised geographical areas and specific needs groups, as undertaken in the former Central Regional Council's Social Strategy (see Chapter 3) is one approach. The ever increasing financial constraints on social housing organisations makes this a daunting task. Nevertheless, if anti-poverty strategies are going to fulfil a significant role, then a social audit approach is needed, whereby existing policies and spending priorities are evaluated in terms of their impact on poverty and social exclusion.

If zero-based budgeting is combined with a social audit, organisations can review critically all their existing policies and practices. Thus this type of approach would provide the basis for social housing organisations to evaluate their core activities.

❑ Monitoring and evaluation

Monitoring and evaluation are often marginalised as stages of strategic management, and they are frequently ignored in much of the public sector policy making process. It is particularly important to monitor and evaluate housing and anti-poverty strategies and activities, since they use new practices where outcomes cannot be predicted from past experience.

There are three basic questions:

- are the activities **meeting the original aims and objectives** of the project? The answer to this will in part depend on the clarity of the original ideas including the precision of the objectives;
- do the activities **have regard to the broader anti-poverty strategies** operating in the locality? This will depend, to a large extent, on the degree of inter-agency working and collaboration; and
- do the activities **contribute to alleviating some of the symptoms** of poverty and social exclusion? This will also mainly depend on whether these symptoms were adequately defined in the first place.

Having developed a framework for evaluation, it is important that housing organisations make explicit attempts to utilise it. Of course, there are some difficulties in doing this, as many projects in this newly developing field are in their early stages. It would thus be inappropriate in such circumstances to carry out a major piece of investigative evaluation. Nevertheless, some detailed evaluative research has been carried out on a few anti-poverty related initiatives. More significantly, and especially relevant for 'welfare to work' initiatives, there is a much richer tradition of evaluative research in the USA and this is referred to in the next chapter.

One of the most interesting examples of a review of a specific initiative is McGregor et al's (1997) evaluation of the Wise Group (see Chapter 6). The research focused on whether the Wise Group programmes in Glasgow and Newham were achieving their original aims and objectives of:

> *"delivering linked physical and economic regeneration in areas of disadvantage through recruiting, training and managing a workforce drawn from the long term unemployed to carry out a range of housing and environmental improvements."*

The report concluded that the programmes had both strengths and weaknesses. In the latter category, it was unclear to what extent the improvement programmes contributed to an improved quality of living for local communities. In relation to strengths, McGregor et al (1997) conclude that:

> *"... the savings in unemployment benefit and the severely disadvantaged client group recruited suggest that the Wise Group provides good value for money."*

A further example of a detailed evaluation of an anti-poverty initiative has been carried out by Gilroy (1996) who studied the Cruddas Park Community Development Trust in Newcastle. The Trust was set up in 1989 as part of the Cruddas Park Initiative to tackle the problems of multiple deprivation on a large local authority housing estate. Her study noted that there was a tendency to focus on quantitative output measures, including 350 long term unemployed people gaining work, and four community businesses being established. She found that it was much more difficult to evaluate the more qualitative aims – such as empowering local people and building social capital. Stakeholders tended to be more interested in the former than in the latter. Yet anti-poverty initiatives are about more than the number of jobs created, and many of the case studies in the previous chapters have pointed to the importance of improving the quality of life of local people.

A further example of evaluative research is Pacione's study of LETS in Glasgow (Pacione, 1997). He contrasts a successful LETS in West Glasgow with an unsuccessful project on Drumchapel Estate. In the latter, there were overwhelming obstacles to the establishment and running of a LETS including – low levels of trust between people on the estate; the conservative nature of the residents; and the attitudes of the Benefits Agency. In the former, the LETS performed important community, economic and social functions which fostered neighbourhood spirit, and clearly was a success. However, as Pacione notes, the West Glasgow LETS was primarily based around a middle class inner suburb rather than a deprived peripheral estate. This obviously raises fundamental questions as to the extent to which such projects are relevant for the most deprived and socially excluded neighbourhoods.

Three initiatives – North Tyneside City Challenge, Western Isles and Skye and Lochalsh Partnership, and Coventry and Warwickshire Partnership Ltd – were evaluated by Geddes and Bennington (1997). They conclude that local regeneration partnerships cannot overcome many of the structural problems of an area but that effective co-ordination and collaboration is essential if realistic aims and objectives are to be achieved.

A further example of policy evaluation is Clapham et al's (1996) study of citizenship and housing for the Chartered Institute of Housing. This research takes a much broader perspective, and examines initiatives undertaken by housing organisations to help to overcome the social exclusion faced by disadvantaged communities, young people and disabled persons. It defines citizenship in terms of promoting skills and abilities, encouraging participation, and enhancing rights and responsibilities. It then evaluates a range of specific activities which have been developed by housing organisations. It concludes that housing organisations are undertaking a wide range of schemes and projects which do enhance citizenship, but external constraints hinder these innovative approaches.

Monitoring and the evaluation of projects and strategies is thus an essential part of the strategy process. Housing organisations need to use existing evaluative research on such initiatives. This will ensure that a realistic assessment is made of the potential of the transfer of ideas as well as the introduction of new initiatives.

Guide to further reading

The following guides are useful on certain external funding sources:

Priority Estates Project (1997): *How to Win Money from the Lottery without Having to Buy a Ticket?*: Manchester, PEP

Stephens M et al (1996): *European Funding – The Independent Social Housing Sector and the European Structural Funds*: London, National Housing Federation

The following give details on evaluation:

Clapham D et al (1996): *Citizenship and Housing*: Coventry, CIH

Geddes M and Bennington J (1997): *Partnership against Poverty and Exclusion?*: Bristol, The Policy Press

McGregor A et al (1997): *Bridging the Jobs Gap*: York, Joseph Rowntree Foundation and York Publishing Services

Pacione M (1997): Local Exchange Trading Systems as a Response to the Globalisation of Capitalism: *Urban Studies* Vol 34 No 8 pp 1179-1199

Chapter 8

Future Directions

This concluding chapter focuses on the relationship between local housing and anti-poverty strategies and the broader economic, political, and social environments including government policies. More specifically, it:

- highlights the consequences of failing to take action on poverty and social exclusion;
- discusses government policies and initiatives for tackling poverty and social exclusion;
- examines, in particular, welfare to work and the social exclusion unit which are government flagship projects; and
- indicates broader action required at national and local levels.

❑ Introduction

Local housing and anti-poverty strategies are not going to solve all the problems of poverty. Even on their own terms, most initiatives have limitations. Reference has already been made to the need for action at the national level to address economic and social trends:

> *"... strategies which target local poverty and local poor people will fail to solve the problems of local poverty because, for all their tactical sophistications and achievements, they are the product of policy failure – the failure to tackle the economic and social policy trends which have led to disinvestment and unemployment."* (Alcock, 1994, p 151.)

The Government's focus on initiatives such as welfare to work, health action zones, education action zones, and the creation of the cabinet unit to co-ordinate interventions on poverty and social exclusion, recognises the need for fundamental change to reduce poverty.

In relation to housing organisations, John Crawley of Birmingham Friendship Housing Association, has commented that 'the only cure for poverty is a fairer distribution of income and wealth' (Crawley, 1996). He argues that housing associations ought to be more modest in describing their roles. National policy changes, such as enhancing benefits by £15 per week and restoring the links between earnings and benefits, would do more to redress poverty than many of the activities being considered by housing organisations.

Similarly, Hutton (1997) argues that 'the solution to social housing's problems has nothing to do with development, management and allocations ... ultimately it is a labour market problem'.

If Hutton is correct, should housing organisations avoid anti-poverty strategies because they deal with symptoms rather than causes? The answer depends on whether they are prepared to make a difference. As providers of goods and services to economically and socially disadvantaged households they have the power to:

- provide sustainable tenancies;
- ensure that their current activities do not worsen the poverty situation;
- redress the effects of poverty where they can; and
- help local people and communities develop greater social cohesion.

As strategic enablers, housing organisations can:

- encourage other organisations to participate in anti-poverty initiatives; and
- contribute to providing the policy and research framework for action.

Thus as Chris Holmes, Director of Shelter, has said:

> *"Housing should be a priority ... But this means far more than just building homes and housing the homeless. It must be at the heart of a new vision which tackles poverty and unemployment, and promotes self-reliant, socially mixed and sustainable communities."* (Holmes, 1997)

❑ Optimistic and pessimistic scenarios

The Director of Policy and Research at Demos, Perri 6, argues:

> *"The fatalism of the socially excluded will not be tackled until we challenge the fatalism of the wider public who have too often been persuaded that there can*

> *never be work for everyone, that mass unemployment is a permanent feature of our lives and that the best the poor can hope for are slightly more generous benefits."* (Perri 6, 1997)

If this fatalism is not attacked, the implications for the 'haves' and 'have nots' are bleak. Writers frequently illustrate the consequences of fatalism and inaction on poverty by adopting a comparative perspective. Although situations may not transfer readily between countries with different socio-economic and political traditions, it is a useful technique for challenging assumptions and perceptions. In the context of poverty and social exclusion, will the future situation in the UK move towards the (pessimistic) North American picture or the (optimistic) North Western European one?

■ The North American situation

Massey (1996) has commented that in the 1990s in the USA (and elsewhere) there have been rising levels of income inequality and segregation. The geographical barriers between the rich and the poor have increased steadily over the last few decades leading to a concentration of problems in certain neighbourhoods. In some USA cities 'moving from a neighbourhood where the poverty rate is under 20% to one where it is about 40% increases the rate of violent crime threefold'. Similarly, a one-point increase in the poverty rate in neighbourhoods in Philadelphia raises the crime rate by 0.8%.

Massey forecasts that the situation will continue to deteriorate and that USA cities will become part of 'the age of extremes' in the early part of the next century. In other words, geographical concentrations of affluence will enhance the benefits and privileges for the rich, while in poor neighbourhoods there will be increased exposure to crime, disease, and violence. He refers to this as 'the hour-glass effect'.

Will these trends also happen in the UK? Hutton suggests that such changes are already taking place. Professor David Donnison in the 1997 Stamp Memorial Lecture argued that the previous government's policies were 'leading us down a ruinous road whose ultimate destination, now clearly visible, can be seen in the American ghettos'. He went on to comment that government must stop trying to evade its housing and taxation responsibilities.

■ The North Western European situation

The situation in USA cities can be contrasted with the picture in countries such as the Netherlands and Sweden. Nevertheless, as Massey (1996) indicates, there is growing evidence of a slow but gradual increased level of social polarisation in many cities in North Western Europe.

A major difference between the USA, the UK, the Netherlands and Sweden is the scale and degree of residualisation of social housing. Table 8.1 shows how much more widely social housing is used in the latter two countries. They have greater economic diversity among social housing tenants, as well as more advocates for it among the population.

Table 8.1: Social rented housing by country

Country	Proportion of social rented households
Netherlands	40%
Sweden	36% (includes 15% co-ops)
UK	23%
USA	5%

Source: Oxley and Smith (1996)

Social housing in the Netherlands and Sweden is not primarily housing for the poor. As a result, the focus of the activities of housing organisations in these two countries is rather different from the UK. Their social housing management has not yet had to address the scale and degree of poverty faced by organisations in the UK.

❑ Government policy

If Britain is to follow the more optimistic trajectory, strong **national** policies to tackle poverty and social exclusion are required which are linked to **local** strategies and actions.

We, of course, need to be clear that poverty and social exclusion are **not** mutually interchangeable terms, even though policy debates often implicitly assume a high degree of similarity. Social exclusion focuses attention on the ways in which groups are excluded from participating in mainstream society through, for example, lack of jobs, poor housing, inadequate access to education and training, and lack of leisure and recreational opportunities. Poverty, on the other hand, is primarily concerned with inadequate individual and/or household income. Thus, those who are defined as poor (or in poverty) may not necessarily be socially excluded, while those who are faced with social exclusion need not lack income (see Appendices for further discussion on this issue).

The Government, since May 1997, has announced a variety of initiatives aimed at tackling both poverty and social exclusion. These initiatives are each at different stages in policy development and implementation. Moreover, they are significant in relation to the activities of housing organisations – as the examples in the following table illustrate.

Table 8.2: Examples of government initiatives to tackle poverty and social exclusion

Government initiative	Nature of initiative	Relevance for housing organisations
Childcare (November 1997)	£300m strategy to provide up to 30,000 new out-of-school clubs and up to one million new childcare places	Housing organisations could support and facilitate schemes (see Chap 6)
Education Action Zones (November 1997)	25 EAZs are initially to be designated to raise educational standards in areas with low educational attainment standards	Housing organisations could usefully work with Local Education Authorities and local communities in drawing up proposals to tackle social and educational disadvantage
Health Action Zones	A limited number of areas are to be designated to tackle health and wider inequality	As above – especially as there is now official recognition for the close relationship between poor health, low incomes and bad housing – see Chap 6
New Deal and Welfare to Work (July 1997)	An initial focus on providing jobs and training for people under 25 who have been on job seekers allowance for more than 6 months. The scheme is being extended during 1998 to long term unemployed, those on invalidity benefits and lone parents	Housing organisations are and can participate in the provision of training and employment initiatives under this programme which is based on competitive bidding. Examples of the types of schemes which might be developed can be found in Chap 6
Social Exclusion Unit (December 1997)	Cabinet Unit aimed at promoting good practice and integrated solutions at national and local level. Initial focus on rough sleepers, problem estates and school exclusions/truancy	Housing organisations should be highlighting good practice and ensuring a co-ordinated partnership approach on problem estates and tackling the issue of homelessness

Later sections of this chapter will focus in more detail on welfare to work and the social exclusion unit. It is, however, also important to appreciate the following points about these initiatives:

- they overlap at the national level, e.g. welfare to work and the new deal link with the childcare initiative (lone parents will be able to take advantage of out-of-school clubs, and the childcare initiative could provide as many as 50,000 unemployed people with training opportunities as childcarers);
- housing organisations must appreciate these national level linkages as well as participating in promoting collaboration at the local scale – organisations must not operate independently; and
- as Chapter 6 has shown, some housing organisations have already developed innovative projects which could usefully be developed and modified to meet specific local circumstances by other housing bodies.

In addition, there will be further government initiatives introduced which will either take the form of extending current projects (e.g. extending the new deal to those on invalidity benefits in late 1998) or new schemes. In both cases, housing organisations ought to be involved in discussing possible action with other bodies now!

These new schemes will be the outcome of nearly 50 government policy reviews which are part of and linked to a series of comprehensive spending reviews. The outcomes of some have been foreshadowed by ministerial speeches and discussion papers. They **might**, for instance, include:

- 'contrats de ville' (city contracts) as an element within the single regeneration budget (SRB) – this is a French concept which puts greater emphasis on tackling housing issues and social exclusion;
- tax and benefit reforms such as:
  - removing entitlement to 100% housing benefit partly as an incentive for people to seek work;
  - attention to tapers and other work disincentives within the benefit system;
  - establishing a system of 'working family tax credits' to reinforce the effects of a minimum wage in combating low pay;
  - introducing a 10p rate of income tax; and
- initiatives on skills and training arising from the deliberations of the Government's skills task force.

Some of these ideas will progress while others will fail to materialise. Housing organisations must keep themselves informed about these events as well as considering the implications for anti-poverty strategies.

So far, this section has highlighted the diverse and varied set of existing and potential government initiatives. But do they add up to a coherent approach for tackling poverty and social exclusion?

Although there has been no single explicit speech or discussion paper, the combination of the July 1997 Budget, the November 1997 pre-Budget statement, and the speeches of the Prime Minister on welfare policy in June 1997 and at the launch of the social exclusion unit in December 1997 indicate the following underpinning principles:

- the main causes of poverty and social exclusion are the lack of a job;
- lack of a job arises from inadequate childcare provision, inappropriate skills or a lack of adequate training, low educational achievement at school;
- a holistic approach is needed by policy makers and service delivery organisations so that the complex nature of the problem is tackled in a co-ordinated manner – 'joined-up solutions to joined-up problems'; and
- higher welfare benefits in real terms (achieved through income redistribution) create welfare dependency and thus social exclusion.

These themes and principles are evident in two of the Government's flagship initiatives – welfare to work and the social exclusion unit. These are critically discussed in the next two sections.

■ Government policy on welfare to work

Welfare to work is not a new idea. Considerable interest in the American equivalent, workfare, was shown by the Conservative Government in the late 1980s. Partly as a result of this, there were (by the mid 1990s) nearly 50 welfare to work programmes operating in the UK. They included training and educational programmes such as employment training and training for work, job search measures (e.g. travel to interview schemes), and public job creation (e.g. Project Work).

However, unlike in the USA, there have been no detailed government-based evaluations of these schemes. The previous Government appeared to have had little intention to scrutinise the impact of these measures and often failed to keep accurate information about the costs and benefits of projects. Gardiner (1997) has attempted to evaluate these schemes and, despite a paucity of data, found:

- only between 2% and 28% of participants found jobs as a direct result of welfare to work schemes;
- gross unit costs of getting people into jobs fell in the range of £1,000 – £10,000 for every additional person in employment; and
- the net financial impact of schemes after one year for each extra person in work ranged from a net saving of £7,000 to a net cost of £8,000.

Not surprisingly, Gardiner concludes that a much greater focus on measuring the effectiveness and value for money of welfare to work policy is required.

Workfare in the USA has been evaluated more thoroughly. There it was found to raise the following issues:

- **discretion** – in the USA, there is considerable local state discretion in the operation of some programmes – especially since legislation in 1996. This has raised concerns over whether local budgets will be adequate to help the significant numbers of poor people onto ladders of opportunity, as well as highlighting the variability between areas in respect of who does and does not benefit.
- **cost of workfare** – it is estimated that the true cost is as much as 60% more than a simple benefits regime because of, for example, state funding for childcare, guaranteed health care for the low paid, and help with travel costs in getting and holding down jobs. In the UK, it is noteworthy that the November 1997 pre-Budget statement included announcements on Government investment in childcare partly to support the 'new deal'.

Both of these first two points suggest the need to evaluate the Government's schemes in the UK on these terms.

- **housing costs and workfare** – first, do housing policies conflict with workfare policies and, second, does workfare promote a low wage economy which will prevent those who get jobs from being able to afford decent housing?

  Housing benefit cuts for young people (such as 'single room rent') undermine the objectives of the 'new deal'. In relation to access to housing, this raises fundamental issues over the minimum wage policy – especially for young people.

- **principles of workfare** – there has been an on-going debate as to the conflicting aspects of workfare – as a means of promoting opportunities on the one hand, and penalising welfare recipients on the other.

  Housing organisations in the UK need to ensure that they focus on the former rather than the latter.

It is, of course, difficult at this stage to evaluate or speculate on the impact of the Government's new deal initiative which was launched in mid 1997 and is being implemented during 1998 and 1999. Nevertheless, the key points of the package and their relevance for housing organisations are:

- the new deal initiative is being funded primarily from the one-off windfall levy on utilities;
- the co-ordinating organisation is the Employment Service;
- there has been immediate emphasis on young people (18-24 years old) who have been claiming job seekers allowance for more than six months. Initially, it provides intensive counselling, guidance and advice for up to four months through the Gateway Project (and this may involve basic skills training). Those who remain unemployed will be offered various options including a six month public or private sector employment option, a one year full time education option, a voluntary sector option, and an environment task force option;
- people who unreasonably turn down options may face benefits sanctions for certain periods;
- the scheme started in 12 pathfinder areas from January 1998 and has been extended to the rest of the country from April 1998;
- local consortia, overseen by the Employment Service, are implementing the projects; and
- further 'new deals' are being developed for other target groups (e.g. those over 25 years who have been unemployed for more than two years, lone parents on benefits and people with disabilities and/or on invalidity benefits), but they have different delivery mechanisms and don't involve the voluntary sector or environment task force options.

Housing organisations **could** play a significant role in implementing the new deal element of welfare to work. However, as was pointed out in Chapter 1, the evidence is that few housing organisations have actively participated so far, despite its relevance for tackling poverty and social exclusion. It is thus imperative that housing organisations consider their involvement within the parameters of their housing and anti-poverty strategies.

❑ Social exclusion cabinet unit

A further government theme is policy co-ordination and collaboration. This is one of the prime purposes of the social exclusion unit within the Cabinet Office. The work of the unit is scheduled to be completed by the end of 1999.

Its relevance for housing organisations cannot be overstated, because two of its initial three targets are housing-orientated:

- problem housing estates – its prime targets are the worst 1,370 social housing estates identified by a range of indicators of deprivation – it is anticipated that the unit will produce a report by late summer 1998;
- rough sleepers – the unit intends to produce a report by late spring 1998; and
- the third target is truancy and school exclusion.

Its approach is to focus on:

- prevention rather than cure;
- co-ordination of existing policies at a national and local level;
- identification and promotion of existing good practice;
- brainstorming about new initiatives; and
- influencing resource allocation by other government departments and external bodies – there is unlikely to be any additional public funding.

Housing organisations which clearly understand the first four of these points – prevention, co-ordination, good practice, and innovation – stand to gain from the fifth. They need to work strategically with local communities and partners to maximise this potential advantage.

Nevertheless, they should consider critically the nature of the Government's initiative, bearing in mind the following points:

- focusing on 1,370 large social housing estates assumes a rather narrow view and misinterpretation of the nature of both poverty and social exclusion. Lee and Murie (1997) point out that the link between social housing and disadvantaged households differs between cities, and that anti-poverty initiatives targeted on council housing exclude some disadvantaged groups, e.g. ethnic minorities in older unimproved housing in inner areas. Furthermore, the use of urban-based indicators of deprivation implies that there is not a rural poverty issue! There is plenty of evidence from bodies such as ACRE, CPAG and Shelter that there is a rural housing and poverty problem;

- the ability of even a special cabinet unit to achieve its aims and influence national and local policies within two years is debatable. This is especially so in a period of fundamental reviews of related policy areas such as the comprehensive spending review and the tax and benefit system; and
- national government initiatives often adopt a top-down approach. It is therefore essential that attempts are made to influence policy from the bottom-up especially from the local community level.

❑ Towards a new national strategy

Thus, while local housing and anti-poverty strategies are important in addressing the symptoms of poverty, and attempting to build up social cohesion from the local neighbourhood level, action is also required at the national level. The Government's initiatives, especially on welfare to work and social exclusion, are to be applauded but not in an uncritical manner. The focus on poverty and social exclusion is welcome after nearly 20 years of neglect, but are the Government's initiatives sufficient and are its values appropriate?

A key message from the previous sections is that local initiatives must be linked to a comprehensive set of ideas and policies at a national level. Housing organisations will recognise that their effectiveness is strongly influenced by the wider economic, social and political context. This section discusses some elements of a more sustainable framework.

The Government has taken a number of steps in the process of reforming the welfare system which will impact on local housing and anti-poverty strategies. There is, in addition, hope that more fundamental changes may be introduced which embrace such ideas as the replacement of housing benefit with housing credit (as urged by the Chartered Institute of Housing in 1997) and a review of the earnings benefit taper.

The scale of reform needed to the welfare system cannot be overestimated. The assumed purpose of welfare policy for many decades was to provide money and services for consumption during brief periods of unemployment and a relatively short period of old age (Mulgan, 1997). A welfare policy is now required which reflects current and future realities such as:

- flexible labour markets, especially short term and part time contracts;
- periods of no employment;
- work as a source of status as well as income; and
- long life after retirement, with lengthening periods of intensive care.

This may necessitate radical long term innovations for the welfare system such as:

- promoting 'life skills' and 'volunteering' rather than providing just money;
- paying agencies to organise labour for domestic tasks such as child care – as happens in the Netherlands;
- promoting work sharing; and
- the government as an employer of last resort.

There are indications that the Government may be partly thinking along these lines. For example, its welfare to work scheme includes an environment task force, and the expansion of the home insulation programme including training for young people. There are obvious and useful parallels here with some of the innovative local schemes mentioned in Chapter 6 (e.g. the Wise Group). However, media coverage of the debates on welfare (together with the content of many ministerial speeches) suggests so far a much narrower and somewhat shallow focus including:

- maintaining, rather than increasing, existing levels of public expenditure;
- cutting welfare benefits in order to fund new schemes covering health, education and training;
- focusing on jobs within the mainstream labour market as the main means of tackling poverty and social exclusion; and
- initiating short term projects with a limited life span.

This hardly suggests a radical welfare reforming government committed to a necessary long term attack on both poverty and social exclusion.

The following section, therefore, focuses attention on a crucial issue underpinning welfare reform – the scale and extent of welfare spending. This is followed by a commentary on some immediate suggestions for a national strategy to tackle poverty, and which would help local housing organisations in implementing their housing and anti-poverty strategies.

❑ Welfare spending

Debates on current and future welfare policy are complex. Government is focusing attention on the scale of welfare spending as it continues to rise. Welfare expenditure has a fundamental impact on low income households and those devising strategies at the local level.

Welfare spending has more than doubled since 1951, from just over 10% of Gross Domestic Product to more than 22%. Within that, spending on the social security budget has nearly tripled, while health and education expenditure has, as a proportion of GDP, grown only marginally. Since 1979 the growth is even more marked. A review of government expenditure figures for social security expenditure suggests 'a juggernaut out of control'. The budget has grown from 23% of government expenditure in 1979 to 31% in 1996. The Department of Social Security (DSS) budget has become the dominant force in government expenditure. Of the 21 government departments, it has a larger budget than the combined budgets of 18 of them.

During the early 1990s the annual budget was consistently overspent, often by £1-2 billion. Politicians feared that they have been 'taken prisoner by the imperial guard at the DSS' (Field, 1996), and this has created difficulties for government in prioritising expenditure across its total spending programme.

While the DSS budget has risen, total government spending has remained largely contained around 22% of GDP. The changes have been in resource shifts within overall welfare spending – with funding moving away from housing and education to social security.

The policy on social security spending in the 1990s had been one of containment. The Government has committed itself to a fundamental review under Frank Field. At the same time, it is reviewing all areas of public expenditure – the comprehensive spending reviews. The main thrust of social security changes, until 1997, was to restrict access to benefits by reducing eligibility, extending means testing and making funding discretionary. These changes added to the poverty trap. The effect on households was to lock both partners into benefits as no single wage has been sufficient to spring the household free – creating the 'two wage – no wage' division (Hutton, 1995).

Actions taken by the Government since May 1997 suggest so far an extension of these principles:

- abolition of lone parent benefits as agreed in December 1997 – despite opposition to this type of initiative before the General Election; and
- consideration during late 1997 to cutting either the availability, or the level, of disability benefits, to fund extra spending on health and education.

In summary the real issue is the shift in expenditure between budgets, in particular the growth in means tested benefits which was encouraged by the previous Government. A former Minister of Housing in 1988 indeed argued that housing benefits should take the strain of higher rents in the social housing sector.

The comprehensive spending reviews need to address the balance between bricks and mortar subsidies and personal subsidies, as well as the apportionment of budgets between departments. They also need to avoid further cuts in welfare services, and offer opportunities to increase investment on housing, education and health, so as to generate future economic prosperity.

❑ Options for change: benefits, taxation and public policy

■ Benefits

The benefits system causes major problems for those on low paid employment or without work, as well as giving them some support. It is highly complex with some 40 different benefits available. Any new welfare system needs to be simple to understand, flexible to cope with a broad range of claimant circumstances, and focused towards encouraging training and employment.

The current interactions between a flexible labour market and tax and benefit system create a benefits trap. Those who are in search of work typically experience a cycle of badly paid employment followed by a period of unemployment. Instead of escaping into stable employment, they continue in the cycle or resign themselves to a life on benefit.

Housing benefit, for example, was established to assist low income households to meet the costs of rented accommodation by targeting benefit to meet rent costs. The housing benefit system, however, has created a poverty trap, where rises in income are affected by almost pound for pound reductions in benefit.

Consideration needs to be given to the creation of a unified housing subsidy covering households on low incomes in all tenures. This debate grew in momentum with the growth in negative equity and mortgage arrears during the early 1990s. The Chartered Institute of Housing has proposed that a housing credit system should replace housing benefit (Wilcox, 1997). The proposals are in two stages. First, a new housing credit system would replace housing benefit, and be applied also to low income home owners. There would be an increase in the earnings disregard and the tariff applied to savings would be halved. The second stage would include harmonising housing benefit and family credit and easing the poverty trap. The cost to the Exchequer would be modest – Wilcox estimates that it could be funded by reducing the rate of MIRAS from 15% to 10%. In July 1997, the Government took this last step but has not yet adopted the housing credit idea.

■ Tax

From 1945, the aim of taxation was not only to generate income for public expenditure, but to act as a wealth redistributor. The tax system changes since 1979 have undermined this principle and deepened inequalities by:

- shifting the tax base from direct taxes to indirect taxes;
- increasing the tax base so bringing more people into tax at the lower end;
- reducing higher rates of tax; and
- increasing the basic rate of national insurance.

The move to indirect taxation has been a key feature of policy, but is highly regressive, as the poorest spend higher proportions of their income on consumption. For the lowest income groups the increases in indirect taxes have not been off set by reductions in direct taxation.

While the tax system needs to avoid disincentives to work, or to create wealth, it also needs to work in hand with anti-poverty initiatives. A review of taxation alongside benefits should aim to share wealth creation, offer opportunities for all and in so doing reduce the gross inequalities in income, health, educational attainment and housing.

❑ Public policy

The tax and benefits systems do not stand in isolation. Public policy can also be used to enhance anti-poverty activities. This section briefly considers three illustrative examples of sustainable policies – a national minimum wage, childcare and training.

■ National minimum wage

Since the 1980s there has been a major debate about the advantages and disadvantages of a national minimum wage. The arguments in favour are based on social justice – ensuring that employees receive the full value of the goods or services they produce. Low pay has become a major contributor to poverty – a comparison of low paid households in poverty over the past decade reveals that the proportions have tripled from 4% to 13% (Webb, 1996). The Low Pay Unit has long argued that the most effective response is to set a national minimum wage.

Counter arguments claim that a national minimum wage reduces employment opportunities. Experience in the European Union countries and the USA demonstrates that a minimum wage policy, if managed effectively, does **not** impact in this way. The key issue is the level of the minimum figure.

The Government has established a low pay commission to recommend a figure. Even so, it should be remembered that a national minimum wage only affects those in work. It does not help those with no wage!

■ Education and childcare

One of the main costs facing lone parents, as well as those households where both partners have jobs, is childcare. If a government is to tackle dependency and reduce welfare expenditure it needs a mechanism which provides adequate low cost childcare. At the same time, there is the need to focus directly on improving educational attainment. The Government White Paper on Education (1997) gave a number of vital commitments including nursery provision for all four year olds and family literacy and numeracy schemes. The November 1997 pre-Budget statement included an announcement of a £300m investment in childcare. The Prime Minister's commitment in December 1997 at the launch of the social exclusion unit to target truancy and school exclusion is a further example of initiatives which have already been taken.

The solution to this is likely to come in a variety of guises. For children of school age, the extension of home work clubs and offering facilities for supervised study or play enables parents to save childcare costs as well as creating jobs, commonly for lone parents. For pre-school children the approach of the present Government ties in with ideas such as encouraging the provision of free nursery places and reducing the school starting age from five to four. Both can be justified on educational grounds – by starting education earlier, performance is likely to be improved, further aiding future national wealth creation in the long term.

A variety of funding routes can complement state resources in this field – including the use of national lottery funding which is being investigated as part of the Government's current review.

■ Training

There has been continued discussion about encouraging those on benefit to return to work. The approach during the early 1990s was to link benefit payments to training or employment, along the lines of workfare. The approach was underpinned by a belief that the key skill required was work habit.

A new approach is needed. The key element, however, must be to focus on skills training for employment or re-skilling people to take on a new area of work. In addition, support must be given to employers to create new jobs to use these new skills which people have developed. Training without employment opportunities is a wasted investment. Hence action is required both on the supply and demand sides of the labour market.

The Government's welfare to work package announced in the July 1997 Budget included proposals to help 250,000 young people on a range of schemes including an environmental task force and home insulation programmes. Local authorities are expected to spend 15% of the resources from the capital receipts initiative on environmental regeneration. Although the scale of activity is impressive in this area, these first proposals will only help 2% of those living in poverty.

❑ Summary and recommendations

The UK economy has seen a growing proportion of expenditure on the welfare state, but it is still lower than comparable nations. Of concern is the growth in expenditure on welfare benefits, particularly means tested benefits, and the loss of expenditure for health, education and housing.

Anti-poverty strategies will have limited local impacts, unless accompanied by a broader national strategy which uses the tax and benefits system to reduce inequality, and which encourages a return to employment through fair wage rates, re-skilling and adequate childcare and education provision.

More immediately, there are a number of specific measures which the government should take to encourage housing organisations to participate in multi-agency housing and anti-poverty approaches involving local communities. The Government has already indicated that it intends to modify legislation so enabling local authorities to introduce local labour contract requirements and hence promote local training and employment as part of urban regeneration schemes. In addition, it should immediately:

- modify the Housing Act 1996, to allow registered social landlords to take on a wider remit of activities than just the development and management of housing;
- enhance the participatory rights of local communities so that they are centrally involved in policies which affect them; and
- ensure the dissemination of locally-based best practice ideas for tackling poverty and social exclusion.

Guide to further reading

A useful summary of the welfare to work and new deal initiatives can be found in Housing Today (1977): *Update – The New Deal*: 30th October

The role and purpose of the social exclusion unit has been debated at length in:
Agenda (October 1997) and *Roof* (November/December 1997)

Thought-provoking material on the future of welfare policy includes:
Hutton W (1997): New Labour, New Levers: *Housing*, May
Mulgan G (1997): Think Well-Being, Not Welfare: *New Statesman*, 17th January
Perri 6 (1997): *Social Exclusion – Time to be Optimistic*: London, Demos Collection 12/1997

More specific material on proposals for reforming the links between housing and welfare include:
Wilcox S (1997): *Replacing Housing Benefit with Housing Credit*: Coventry, CIH
Wilcox S and Sutherland H: *Housing Benefit, Affordability and Work Incentives: Options for Reform*: London, NHF

References and Further Reading

❑ Chapter 1: Tackling Poverty and Social Exclusion

The Garths Estate, Sunderland

Blake J (1995): Moving into Quality Street: *Roof*, September/October

Malpass P and Jones C (1995): *Home Housing Association – A History*: Newcastle, Home Housing Association

Nuttgens P (1989): *The Home Front*: London, BBC Publications

Sherratt C (1995): Rebirth for the Garths: *Housing Review* Vol 44 No 4

Housing Plus

Kemp R and Fordham G (1997): *Going the Extra Mile – Implementing 'Housing Plus' on Five London Housing Association Estates*: York, Joseph Rowntree Foundation and York Publishing Services

The Housing Corporation (1997): *A Housing Plus Approach to Achieving Sustainable Communities*: London, The Housing Corporation

Power A with Richardson L (1996): *Housing Plus – An Agenda for Social Landlords?*: London, London School of Economics

Indicators of poverty and deprivation and resource allocation

Department of the Environment, Transport and the Regions (1997): *Consultation Paper on Proposals for Implementing the Government's Capital Receipts Initiative*: London, DoE

Department of the Environment (1994): *Index of Local Conditions*: London, DoE

Department of the Environment (1995): *Consultation Paper on the Review of the GNI and HNI*: London, DoE

Gordon D and Forrest R (1995): *People and Places 2 – Social and Economic Distinctions in England*: Bristol, School for Advanced Urban Studies

General references

Alcock P (1994): Welfare Rights and Wrongs – The Limits of Local Anti-Poverty Strategies: *Local Economy* Vol 9 No 2

Barrow M and Bachan R (1997): *The Real Cost of Poor Homes*: London, RICS

Chartered Institute of Housing (1995): *A Point to Prove*: Coventry, CIH

Clapham D et al (1996): *Citizenship and Housing – Shaping the Debate*: Coventry, CIH

Department of the Environment (1995): *Our Future Homes*: London, HMSO, Chp 6

Hatchett W (1996): Housing – Local Strategies can ensure Dignity of Full Citizenship: *Housing*, July/August, p13

Hutton W (1995): *The State We're In*: London, Jonathan Cape

Hutton W (1997a): *The State to Come*: London, Vintage Press

Hutton W (1997b): Stakeholding and its Critics: London, IEA *Choice in Welfare* No 36

Hutton W (1997c): New Labour, New Levers: *Housing*, May, pp 24-25

Jowell R et al (Eds) (1995): *British Social Attitudes – The 12th Report*: London, Dartmouth Publishing Company

Passmore J and Ferguson S (1994): *Customer Service in a Competitive Environment*: Coventry, CIH

Wilcox S et al (1993): *Local Housing Companies*: York and Coventry, JRF and CIH

Wilkinson R (1996): *Unhealthy Societies – The Afflictions of Inequality*: London, Routledge

❑ Chapter 2: Poverty and Housing

Berthoud R and Kempson E (1992): *Credit and Debt in Britain*: London, Policy Studies Institute

Bramley G (1991): *Bridging the Affordability Gap in 1990*: Birmingham, BEC Publications

Brown T and Passmore J (1995): *Minority Ethnic Communities' Access to Shared Ownership Housing*: Sevenoaks, Moat Housing Group

Brown T and Passmore J (1996): *Poverty and Social Housing*: Sevenoaks, Moat Housing Group

Burrows R (1997): *Contemporary Patterns of Residential Mobility in Relation to Social Housing in England*: York, Centre for Housing Policy, University of York

Carey S (1995): *Private Renting in England 1993/94*: London, HMSO

Chartered Institute of Housing (1995): Meeting Housing Needs in the Private Rented Sector: *Good Practice Briefing No 1*, March: Coventry: CIH

Chartered Institute of Housing (1997): *Sustainable Home Ownership – New Policies for a New Government*: Coventry, CIH
Chartered Institute of Housing (1997): *Sustainable Home Ownership – The Debate*: Coventry, CIH
Coles A and Taylor B (1993): Trends in Tenure Preference: *Housing Finance* No 19, August
Davey J (1997): What Equity Release Will Pay For?: *Housing Review* Vol 46 No 3
Dennehy A et al (1997): *Not to be Ignored – Young People, Poverty and Health*: London, CPAG
Department of the Environment (1995): *Our Future Homes*: London, HMSO
Department of Social Security (1993): *Households Below Average Incomes*: London, HMSO
Green H et al (1997): *Housing in England 1995/96*: London, HMSO
Holmans A (1996): Meeting Housing Needs in the Private Rented Sector? In Wilcox S (Ed) (1996): *Housing Finance Review 1996/97*: York, Joseph Rowntree Foundation
Kempson E (1996): *Life on a Low Income*: York, Joseph Rowntree Foundation
Kempson E (1993): *Household Budgets and Housing Costs*: London, Policy Studies Institute
Leather P and Mackintosh S (1997): Towards Sustainable Policies for Housing Renewal in the Private Sector. In Williams P (Ed) (1997): *Directions in Housing Policy*: London, Paul Chapman Publishing
Leather P and Morrison T (1997): *The State of UK Housing*: Bristol, The Policy Press
Malpass P and Murie A (1994): *Housing Policy and Practice*: London, Macmillan, 4th Edition
Office for National Statistics (1996): *Family Spending 1995-96*: London, HMSO
Oppenheim C and Harker L (1996): *Poverty – The Facts*: London, CPAG
Page D (1993): *Building Communities*: York, Joseph Rowntree Foundation
Power A with Richardson L (1996): *Housing Plus – An Agenda for Social Landlords?*: London, London School of Economics
Power S et al (1995): *No Place to Learn*: London, Shelter
Wilcox S (Ed) (1996): *Housing Finance Review 1996/97*: York, Joseph Rowntree Foundation
Wilcox S (Ed) (1994): *Housing Finance Review 1994/95*: York, Joseph Rowntree Foundation
Yanetta A and Edwards L (1996): Homelessness and Access to Housing. In Currie H and Murie A (Eds) (1996): *Housing in Scotland*: Coventry, CIH

❑ Chapter 3: Acting Strategically

Alcock P et al (1995): *Combating Local Poverty – The Management of Anti-Poverty Strategies by Local Government*: Luton, LGMB

Audit Commission (1992): *Developing Local Authority Housing Strategies*: London, HMSO

Ball R and Higgins V (1996): The Management and Development of Anti-Poverty and Social Strategies. In *Local Government Policy Making* Vol 22 No 5

Bowman A (1995): *Models of Collaboration – The Experience of Neighbourhood Transformation in the USA*: Baltimore, John Hopkins University

Burton P (1993): *Community Profiling*: Bristol, School for Advanced Urban Studies

Catterick P (1995): *Business Planning for Housing*: Coventry, CIH

Chartered Institute of Housing (1997): *Good Practice Briefing No 7 – Local Housing Strategies*: Coventry, CIH

Clapham D et al (1991): *Community Ownership in Glasgow*: Edinburgh, Scottish Office Central Research Unit

Fraser R (1990): *Working Together in the 1990s*: Coventry, CIH

Gibson T (1993): *Danger – Opportunity – A Report to the Joseph Rowntree Foundation on Meadowell Community Development*: London, Neighbourhood Initiatives Foundation

Gibson T (1997): *Power in Our Hands*: London, Jon Carpenter

Gordon D and Forrest R (1993 and 1995): *People and Places I and II*: Bristol, School for Advanced Urban Studies

Hawtin M et al (1994): *Community Profiling*: Buckingham, Open University Press

Hudson B (1987): Collaboration in Social Welfare: *Policy and Politics* Vol 15 No 3

Lee P and Murie A (1997): *Poverty, Housing Tenure and Social Exclusion*: Bristol, The Policy Press

London Research Centre (1996): *The Capital Divided – Mapping Poverty and Social Exclusion*: London, London Research Centre

Lund B and Foord M (1997): *Towards Integrated Living?*: Bristol, The Policy Press

Percy-Smith J (Ed) (1996): *Needs Assessments in Public Policy*: Buckingham, Open University Press

Ratcliffe P (1996): *'Race' and Housing in Bradford*: Bradford, Bradford Housing Forum

Scottish Homes (1991): *Scottish Homes Statistical Report 1990-91*: Edinburgh, Scottish Homes

Webb A (1991): Co-ordination – A Problem in Public Sector Management: *Policy and Politics* Vol 19 No 4

Willis J (1991): Line of Action on Poverty: *Local Government Chronicle*, 18 October

❑ Chapter 4: Housing Management and Anti-Poverty Initiatives

CIH (1996): *Housing Management Standards Manual*: Coventry, CIH

Kempson E (1995): *Money Advice and Debt Counselling*: London, Policy Studies Institute

Kempson E et al (1994): *Hard Times – How Poor Families Make Ends Meet*: London, Policy Studies Institute

Leicester City Council (1996a): *Get in Touch Not in Debt – Fair Debt Collection Strategy – Officers and Members Handbook*: Leicester, Leicester CC.

Local Government Information Unit (1995): *The Anti-Poverty Implications of Local Government Re-Organisation*: London, LGIU

Power A (1991): *Housing Management – A Guide to Quality and Creativity*: Harlow, Longman

Saunders R (1997): *Resident Service Organisations*: Manchester, PEP

Welsh Federation of Housing Associations (1997): *Housing Association Rents – Disaster?, Crisis?, or What?*: Cardiff, WFHA

Willis J (1991): Line of Action on Poverty: *Local Government Chronicle*, 18 October

❑ Chapter 5: Housing Development and Anti-Poverty Initiatives

Brown T (1994): *Housing and Affordability*: Leicester, Leicester City Council

CIH (1996): *Good Practice Briefing Issue No 6 – Energy Efficiency*: Coventry, CIH

Dean C (1995): From Consultation to Delegation – Economic Regeneration on a Housing Estate: *Local Economy* Vol 9 No 4

Hart J and McGettigan A (1997): *We're All In It Together*: London, Community Self-Build Agency

Holman B (1997): *FARE Dealing – Neighbourhood Involvement in a Housing Scheme*: London, Community Development Foundation

Leicester City Council (1996b): *Home Energy Conservation Act Report*: Leicester, Leicester City Council

Lowe R et al (1996): *Directory of Energy Efficient Housing*: Coventry, CIH

McArthur A et al (1996): *Less than Equal? – Community Organisations and Estate Regeneration Partnerships*: Bristol, The Policy Press

Millar B (1997): From Hard-to-Let to Desirable Docklands: *Housing*, February

National Energy Agency (1997): *Energy Advice for Ethnic Minority Households*: Newcastle, NEA

Poverty Matters (1993): Cold Comfort or Energy Efficiency: *Poverty Matters*, Summer

Taylor L (1993): *Energy Efficient Homes*: Coventry, CIH
Taylor M (1995): *Unleashing the Potential – Bringing Residents to the Centre of Regeneration*: York, Joseph Rowntree Foundation
Whyley C et al (1997): *Fuel Poverty in Europe*: London, Policy Studies Institute

❑ Chapter 6: Anti-Poverty Initiatives and the Community

ABCUL (1993): *Credit Unions – It's for You*: London, Association of British Credit Unions
Cunninghame C et al (1995): *Water Metering*: London, Save the Children
Dean C (1995): From Consultation to Delegation – Economic Regeneration on a Housing Estate: *Local Economy* Vol 9 No 4
Edwards R (1992): Coordination and Definition of Need – The New Under Fives Initiative and Homeless Families: *Children and Society* Vol 6 No 4.
Fitch M (1995): Prepayment for Household Essentials: *Poverty Matters*, Autumn
Hart J and McGettigan A (1997): *We're All In It Together*: London, Community Self-Build Agency
Housing Association Weekly (1995): Enterprising Move: *HA Weekly*, 5 July 1995.
Laughlin S and Black D (1995): *Poverty and Health – Tools for Change*: Birmingham, Public Sector Health Alliance
Local Government Information Unit (1995): *The Anti-Poverty Implications of Local Government Re-Organisation*: London, LGIU
McGregor A et al (1997): *Bridging the Jobs Gap*: York, Joseph Rowntree Foundation and York Publishing Services
McGregor A et al (1995): *Building Futures – Can Local Employment be Created from Housing Expenditure?*: Bristol, School for Advanced Urban Studies
Passmore J (1995): Cleaning up with Water Metering: *Housing*, May
People for Action 2001 (1996): *Good Practice Notes and Factsheets*: Blackheath, People for Action
Poverty Matters (1993): Budgeting without Banks: *Poverty Matters*, Summer
Saunders R (1997): *Resident Service Organisations*: Manchester, PEP
Sheppard E (Ed) (1996): *LETS Info Pack*: Warminster, Letslink
Taylor M (1995): *Unleashing the Potential – Bringing Residents to the Centre of Regeneration*: York, Joseph Rowntree Foundation
Thomas I and Balloch S (1994): *The Expansion of Credit Unions in English Metropolitan Areas 1991-93*: London, AMA
Tickell J (1992): *America's Community Developers and the Empowerment Debate*: London, Report to the Commonwealth Foundation

Wales Cooperative Centre (1995): *Credit unions and the Rural Economy*: Cardiff, Wales Cooperative Centre
Wheway R and Millward A (1997): *Child's Play – Facilitating Play on Housing Estates*: Coventry, CIH
Willis J (1991): Line of Action on Poverty: *Local Government Chronicle*, 18 October

❑ Chapter 7: Resources

Catterick P (1995): *Business Planning for Housing*: Coventry, CIH
Chapman M et al (1994): *Scottish Housing and Europe*: Edinburgh, Scottish Homes, Unpublished Paper
Clapham D et al (1996): *Citizenship and Housing*: Coventry, CIH
Geddes M and Bennington J (1997): *Partnership against Poverty and Exclusion*: Bristol, The Policy Press
Gilroy R (1996): Building Routes to Power – Lessons from Cruddas Park: *Local Economy*, November
McGregor A et al (1997): *Bridging the Jobs Gap*: York, Joseph Rowntree Foundation and York Publishing Services
Pacione M (1997): Local Exchange Trading Systems as a Response to the Globalisation of Capitalism: *Urban Studies* Vol 34 No 8
Power A with Richardson L (1996): *Housing Plus – An Agenda for Social Landlords?*: London, London School of Economics
Stephens M et al (1996): *European Funding – The Independent Social Housing Sector and the European Structural Funds*: London, National Housing Federation

❑ Chapter 8: Future Directions

Alcock P (1994): Welfare Rights and Wrongs – The Limits of Local Anti-Poverty Strategies: *Local Economy* Vol 9 No 2
Crawley J (1996): Office Cleaner is Your Litmus Test: *Agenda*, October
Field F (1996): *How to Pay for the Future*: London, Institute of Community Studies
Gardiner K (1997): *Bridges from Benefit to Work – A Review*: York, York Publishing Services for JRF
Holmes C (1997): Backdoor: *Roof*, May/June
Hutton W (1995): *The State We're In*: London, Jonathan Cape
Hutton W (1997): New Labour, New Levers: *Housing*, May

Lee P and Murie A (1997): *Poverty, Housing Tenure and Social Exclusion*: Bristol, The Policy Press

Massey D (1996): The Age of Extremes – Concentrated Affluence and Poverty in the Twenty-First Century: *Demography* Vol 33 No 4

Mead L (1997): *From Welfare to Work*: London, Institute for Economic Affairs

Mulgan G (1997): Think Well-Being, Not Welfare: *New Statesman*, 17th January

National Housing Federation (1997): Update – The New Deal: *Housing Today*, 30th October

Oxley M and Smith J (1996): *Housing Policy and Rented Housing in Europe*: London, E and F N Spon

Perri 6 (1997): *Social Exclusion – Time to be Optimistic*: London, Demos Collection 12/1997

Webb A et al (1996): *The Changing Face of Low Pay in Britain*: Bath, University of Bath.

Wilcox S (1997): *Replacing Housing Benefit with Housing Credit*: Coventry, CIH

Wilkinson R (1996): *Unhealthy Societies*: London, Routledge

Appendix 1

Housing and Social Policy

The relationship between housing and social policy has undergone a fundamental transformation over the last 50 years. The Beveridge Report, 1942, identified the five great social evils of – squalor, disease, ignorance, idleness, and want. It provided a significant impetus for a comprehensive welfare system, after the Second World War. Both poor housing and poverty were central to the debate in terms of squalor and want. Housing policy, and especially the provision of council housing, was regarded as an important element of the welfare state. But, by the end of the 1980s, housing policy had become a 'wobbly pillar on the fringe of social policy' in many Western European countries (Torgersen, 1987).

Housing policy has become detached from mainstream social policy. This is illustrated in the *12th Report of the British Social Attitudes Survey* (1995) in which 60% of respondents said that the Government 'should increase taxes and spend more on health, education and social benefits'. But the survey also showed that while extra spending on health was a first or second priority for 70% of respondents, only 20% considered extra spending on housing to be a high priority. Health and education may still be regarded as universal welfare services, but housing is now seen as a residual social policy function.

This perception stems in part from a misunderstanding of the nature of housing policy, which is popularly considered to cover only social housing provision. Policy is associated with low quality housing for the poor who have little political influence. As a former Director of Housing for a large metropolitan district has commented, the image of social housing is 'housing for the bad, mad and sad'.

The role of housing policy is, however, much wider than the provision of social housing. It encompasses, for example, policies for older housing areas of owner occupied and private rented accommodation. But both public opinion and Government policy currently presume that home owners and landlords, rather than the state, should be responsible for the upgrading of the stock.

Similarly most housing organisations are directly and indirectly involved in meeting the needs of homeless people. But there is a belief that some homeless people are undeserving of help and support, as illustrated in the debate between 1994 and 1996 on the previous Government's policies, which focused on a narrow definition of 'providing help for those who need it' (see Department of the Environment, 1995).

The weak ties between housing and other areas of social policy, including tackling poverty, have serious ramifications. However, there is a resurgence of interest in the relationship between housing and social policy, including poverty, as five examples show:

Firstly, the *British Medical Journal* has published four special editions since 1995 on inequalities in health, as well as a series of eight articles in 1997 on the relationship between deprivation and health. One of these articles suggests:

> *"Income inequality has spillover effects on society at large, including increased rates of crime and violence, impeded productivity and economic growth, and the impaired functioning of representative democracy. Reduced income inequality offers the prospect of greater social cohesiveness and societal well-being."*
> (Kawachi and Kennedy, 1997)

Secondly, housing provides important examples of the links between low incomes and poor health (Wilkinson, 1996). Not only does damp housing contribute directly to the excess of respiratory diseases, but housing insecurity affects health through predominantly psychosocial channels. Thus rent arrears, mortgage repossessions and temporary accommodation may not only create financial and material insecurity but also stresses which contributes to weakened immunity, less healthy lifestyles and generally poorer health.

Thirdly, and equally significantly, the Chartered Institute of Housing (1995) commented:

> *"Housing problems do not sit in isolation from educational problems or health problems or crime problems or employment problems. The effects all interact and often compound each other. Solutions can only be found by agencies working together and devising strategies which encompass the full spectrum of problems."*

Fourthly, a report by Shelter in 1995 pointed out that 'thousands of children's education is undermined by homelessness' (Power, 1995). More specifically it noted that firstly, children in bed and breakfast accommodation have nowhere to do their homework. Secondly, that children in homeless households faced the disruption of frequent school moves. And thirdly, that there was little evidence of good practice on liaison between housing organisations and education authorities.

Finally, and more generally, housing plus is focused not on housing as a stand alone activity:

> *"Social housing providers operate to tackle the housing provision part of a much bigger and more complex set of needs like education, employment, health and so on."* (Power and Richardson, 1996)

Several registered social landlords have become involved in housing plus activities, including:

Enterprise 5 Housing Association in the North East helped to set up a credit union for its tenants in the early 1990s mainly because they did not qualify for credit cards or loans from reputable lenders.

South London Family Association in the early 1970s worked with Deptford City Challenge and Deptford Task Force on a programme of vocational training and 'local labour in construction' scheme.

Banks of the Wear Housing Association, a member of the Housing 21 Group, have helped form a community development trust in North Sunderland which will be used in part to convert a vacant college building for local activities.

Some of these initiatives stem from the People for Action project which was set up by two housing associations in 1990 with funding from the Wates Foundation and the Department of the Environment in a broadly-based neighbourhood regeneration approach, and by early 1995, 14 housing associations were involved. Other registered social landlords have developed initiatives which can be considered as part of housing plus through establishing projects to ensure long term sustainability of communities.

During the first half of 1997, two large housing associations announced more fundamental restructuring of their organisations. English Churches Housing Group announced in May its intention to move away from development towards 'services and solutions', while the Focus Housing Group indicated that it was exploring ways of transforming itself into a social investment agency to relieve poverty and to regenerate communities.

It would be over-optimistic to suggest that housing policy and practice has a more central place in social policy in the late 1990s. However, there is some evidence of a growing interest in tackling positively the relationships between housing, health, education, employment and poverty. Housing and anti-poverty strategies need to be located within this framework.

References and further reading

Beveridge Report (1942): *Social Insurance and the Allied Services*: London, HMSO

Chartered Institute of Housing (1995): *A Point to Prove*: Coventry, CIH

Council of Churches for Britain and Ireland (1997): *Unemployment and the Future of Work – An Enquiry for the Churches*: London, CCBI

Department of the Environment (1995): *Our Future Homes*: London, HMSO, Chap 6

Jowell R et al (Eds) (1995): *British Social Attitudes – The 12th Report*: London, Dartmouth Publishing Company

Power A with Richardson L (1996): *Housing Plus – An Agenda for Social Landlords?*: London, London School of Economics

Power S et al (1995): *No Place to Learn*: London, Shelter

Torgersen U (1987): Housing – The Wobbly Pillar under the Welfare State. In Turner B et al (Eds) (1987): *Between State and Market*: Stockholm, Almqvist and Wiksell

Wilcox S et al (1993): *Local Housing Companies*: York and Coventry, JRF and CIH

Wilkinson R (1996): *Unhealthy Societies – The Afflictions of Inequality*: London, Routledge

Appendix 2

Poverty – Causes and Impacts

❑ Introduction

This Appendix provides an overview of the causes and effects of poverty in the UK. It:

- defines the complex concept of poverty;
- provides an overview of the literature on the causes of poverty;
- describes the effects of poverty; and

Appendix 3 provides more information on defining and measuring poverty.

It is essential that housing organisations and their staff are familiar with these debates and the terminology so that they can engage in debates with key policy makers and other organisations.

❑ Defining poverty

The European Union Council of Ministers' definition states that poverty occurs where:

> *"persons, families and groups of persons whose resources (material, cultural, social) are so limited as to exclude them from the minimum acceptable way of life in the Member State in which they live."*

There is, however, a vast array of terminology that is associated with the concept of poverty including:

- absolute and relative poverty;
- deprivation;
- new poverty;

- social exclusion and extreme social exclusion; and
- the underclass.

Similarly, there are an equally varied set of concepts used to describe the broad principles for tackling poverty including:

- community and citizenship;
- social justice;
- communitarianism;
- stakeholding; and
- social capital;

In the late 1990s, there is increasing interest in reinventing concepts of *community and citizenship* and putting them into practice. The current Government has frequently stressed the importance of these principles. Tony Blair in his welfare to work speech on the Aylesford Estate in Southwark in June 1997 commented that 'the poorest people have been forgotten by Government' and went on to say:

> *"... fatalism and not just poverty is the problem we face ... a radical shift in values and attitudes is required ... and the message for the next decade is 'we are all in this together' ".*

While Hilary Armstrong, the Minister of Housing, in May 1997 commented:

> *"You cannot deliver an effective housing policy from Whitehall. Policies will only work if they are implemented with the people providing the housing and the people living in them, working together. ... We want to support associated regeneration projects that contribute to the establishment and maintenance of successful communities."*

And in August 1997, Peter Mandelson, as Minister without Portfolio, announced the creation of a new cabinet unit to co-ordinate policy development in tackling poverty. This covers a range of employment and education actions aimed at reducing social exclusion.

These actions and attitudes are closely related to the ideas in a number of influential reports on the future of welfare as well as the writings of leading figures on the future direction of society. Key among them are:

- The Borrie Commission (1994) on **social justice**. This draws attention to the need to move welfare away from a 'safety net to a springboard for economic opportunity'. In particular it emphasises the importance of access to training and employment and the requirement to rebuild the 'social wealth' of the UK.

- Etzioni (1995 and 1997) and **communitarianism**. This focuses on 'a shoring up of our moral responsibilities' including striking a balance between rights and responsibilities, a greater role for the family, and the development of strong social networks.
- Hutton (1995, 1997a, 1997b, 1997c) and **stakeholding**. This emphasises the need to develop a socially cohesive and economically productive system. It requires a democratised welfare state which is more accountable to users. In relation to the housing crisis, he argues that it is ultimately a labour market problem, but that it is also affected by the manner in which the benefits system intersects with housing costs of households, i.e. the poverty trap.
- Putnam (1992) and **social capital**. This draws attention to the importance of a dense network of social organisations, social networks, trust, and shared values in enhancing democratic accountability and economic prosperity.

These and other writers focus on what is needed to transform societies that are facing a downward spiral of decline, i.e. how to move from social exclusion and collapse to social inclusion. Housing organisations are only too aware of these issues in relation to problem estates, run-down inner city areas and socially excluded and disadvantaged groups.

The Chartered Institute of Housing in June 1996 launched a report on citizenship and housing (Clapham et al, 1996). This highlighted a wide range of relevant activities that many housing organisations were already undertaking, and incorporate the principles of:

- promoting rights and respect;
- developing skills and abilities; and
- encouraging active community involvement.

Their activities had a significant role in alleviating social problems including poverty, but there were many obstacles, including society's fixation with a narrow financial definition of value for money. The Editor of *Housing* in reviewing this publication commented that it:

> *"... challenges people working in housing to take a broader view of their work, and to question whether it helps people to become fuller citizens or not. Now there's an issue to put on your next management team agenda!"* (Hatchett, 1996)

❑ Measuring poverty

The topic is made more bewildering and complex by the large number of measures of poverty which are used. They include:

- **quantitative measures** based on official statistics such as Government publications on 'households below average income' and previously 'low income families'; and
- more **qualitative measures** associated with the adequacy of household incomes as determined through opinion poll surveys, e.g. 'Breadline Britain' approach.

These minefields of definitions and measures have usefully been explored by Alcock (1993), Oppenheim and Harker (1996) and Roll (1993). They conclude, for instance, that:

- poverty is a controversial topic representing a 'call-to-action', i.e. it is policy and action orientated;
- policies for tackling poverty reflect different political traditions;
- it is a fruitless task to search for a unitary definition of and a single measure of poverty – defining and measuring poverty is a political issue rather than an objective academic exercise;
- in the UK there is no official poverty line (unlike some other countries) although the Government publishes a range of statistical information on low incomes; and
- debates on the nature and extent of poverty are closely associated with issues of inequality.

More details on these issues can be found in Appendix 3. The controversial nature of the topic is illustrated by the conflict between the previous Government and the Child Poverty Action Group in Spring 1996. The United Nations declared 1996 as the International Year for the Eradication of Poverty. Despite being a signatory to the UN's Copenhagen Declaration in 1995, the Government indicated that it would not set targets to reduce inequality.

The Child Poverty Action Group highlighted that nearly a quarter of the population lived on or below the level of income support, and that 25% of the population had an income, after housing costs, of less than half the national average (Oppenheim and Harker, 1996). More worryingly this latter figure had increased from less than 10% of the population in 1990 to 25% by 1996.

These opposing views reflect different interpretations of poverty. The previous Government was using an absolute definition focusing on the lack of resources to maintain health and basic effective bodily functioning. Thus it was not surprising that the Secretary of State for Social Security highlighted, using information from the Government's Family Expenditure Survey and General Household Survey, how the bottom 20% of the population had acquired more consumer goods over the last two decades. The Child Poverty Action Group, however, adopted a relative approach involving an analysis of the gap between the contented majority and the poor.

Different interpretations and measures of poverty result in markedly different approaches to policy and action. The Director of the Child Poverty Action Group in 1996 called for initiatives which:

- reverse the recent social security cuts;
- move away from tax cuts which transfer income from the poor to the rich; and
- reduce the new insecurities such as negative equity, mortgage arrears and repossessions caused by the flexible labour market.

(Witcher S in the Foreword to Oppenheim and Harker, 1996)

The Secretary of State for Social Security, however, refused to admit the existence of poverty. He argued that it was the personal failings of individuals which contributed to their lack of well-being and hence these victims were part of the undeserving poor for which the state had no responsibility.

Definitions of poverty, such as that of the European Union Council of Ministers, do not resolve the complex issues of the identification and measurement of this phenomenon. They are, nevertheless, useful in setting certain parameters, and in the case of the EU definition there are three basic components:

- poverty affects individuals, households and communities;
- poverty involves not just the lack of financial resources but also the lack of social and cultural resources which prevents participation in wider society; and
- tackling poverty involves the establishment of a set of specific minimum standards.

❑ Causes of poverty

The controversial nature of the debate is partly due to different political beliefs and philosophies.

Alcock (1993), for example, distinguishes between those who favour an **absolute definition** as against those who favour a relative approach to poverty. The former argue that redistributive social policies, including attempts to tackle the consequences of a relative definition of poverty, push up the cost of public expenditure and destroy the incentives of individuals to provide for themselves and their families, so creating a dependency culture.

Supporters of a **relative definition** of poverty, however, argue that what causes poverty is not primarily individual action but 'the dynamics of social and economic forces which structure the production and distribution of resources' (Alcock, 1993). Poverty, as part of the inequality of rewards, is thus the outcome of these forces. Anti-poverty initiatives are thus an attempt to offset the symptoms of relative poverty rather than tackling the causes.

Some, however, are critical of the 'no fault theory that holds sway among the social affairs intelligentsia' (Dennis, 1997). They argue that there has been no increase in poverty, and that the rise of social disorder and the breakdown of communities are due to the decline of the traditional family and the abandonment of male commitment to marriage and parenthood. In other words, poverty and social disorder cannot be attributed to the dynamics of social and economic forces. In many respects such views coincide with those of Murray (1996) who argues that there is an emerging undeserving British underclass, characterised by geographical concentrations of lone parent families, high crime rates, and low levels of employment. Generous welfare benefits have created a culture of dependency which is transmitted across generations. The solutions are based around rebuilding traditional social institutions such as the family and reducing the role of the state.

These perspectives have influenced the debates on so-called problem estates. Page (1993 and 1994) in his research on new housing association estates showed, for example, that new tenants were younger, on lower incomes, less likely to have a job and more likely to be wholly dependent on state benefits than those housed previously. Power and Tunstall (1997) found that, on the local authority estates where there had been serious problems of civil disorder and riots in 1991, there was a 'dangerous combination of large numbers of out-of-work young males with no status or stake in society, people living on low incomes, and households living in areas suffering from a high degree of social stigma'. The collection and analysis of such information contributes to the debates and discussions on aspects of poverty and poor housing, and it is useful to link such research to the wider political debates about the nature and causes of poverty.

The Garths Estate in Sunderland was described in the first chapter. The causes for its decline could be attributed, depending on one's political outlook, to either of these two perspectives.

The Garths Estate, Sunderland

Dynamics of Social and Economic Forces Scenario

In many respects, the estate in the early 1990s had similar characteristics to Page's new housing association estates in that over 50% of new lettings were to people under 25, 90% were on housing benefit, and nearly 70% were unemployed. It could be argued, therefore, that there was an increasing degree of relative poverty and that this was the result of longer term changes in the labour market and the local economy including the loss of traditional manufacturing and construction jobs. Furthermore, changing demographic patterns created the need for more accommodation for young people and smaller households which could only be provided on estates, such as the Garths, where there were relatively high turnover and void rates.

The Underclass Scenario

The increasing level of crime and vandalism culminating in a series of disturbances in November 1993, the unpopularity of the estate among potential tenants with any degree of choice, and the high levels of welfare benefits, could be attributed to the over-generous state welfare system which created a growing culture of dependency among new tenants and the gradual loss of traditional social institutions such as the family. Hence the problems of the Garths Estate could not be attributed to relative poverty.

❑ Effects and extent of poverty

Poverty is a controversial subject. There is no consensus on definitions, measurements or even, its very existence! Nevertheless, there is agreement that phenomenon such as the breakdown of communities and the impact of inequality exist. If one accepts that relative poverty does exist, there is evidence that its scale and extent has increased over the last 20-25 years. The effects can be illustrated in a number of ways including, firstly, through the relationship between poverty, health, housing, education and diet. Secondly, its effects can be examined in relation to its impact on different groups. Finally, there is the geographical dimension to the effects of poverty. However, before briefly dealing with these three aspects, it is important to summarise the extent of poverty in the UK.

The extent of poverty and inequality has been growing over the last two decades. This is after the period in the 1950s and early 1960s when it was generally thought that the giant of poverty had been slain. Research, such as that by Abel-Smith and Townsend (1965), broke this illusion.

While the UK has no official poverty line, the following measurements indicate a growing trend of inequality and poverty:

- the number of people with **incomes below income support level** rose from 3.17 million in 1979 to 4.74 million in 1992. (DSS statistics and House of Commons Social Security Select Committee);
- the number of people living **on or below 50% of average incomes** after housing costs increased from 5 million in 1979 to 13.7 million in 1993/94, from 9% to 25% of the population;
- according to Townsend (1996), the **weekly disposable income** after housing costs for households with children at April 1995 prices were:

Table Appendix 2.1: Disposable income (per week)

	1979	1992/93
Poorest 20%	£88	£78
Richest 20%	£232	£359

- research by Bradshaw (1993) found that **Income Support** met only 75% of the low cost budget for households with two adults and two children, and a lone parent and two children; and
- the Joseph Rowntree Foundation inquiry into *Income and Wealth* (1995) found that **income inequality** grew rapidly between 1977 and 1990 and that over this period 20-30% of the population failed to benefit through the trickle down effects of economic growth.

❑ Relationship between poverty, health, housing and education

The links between housing and poverty are well known. The most striking feature is the relationship between income and tenure.

Table Appendix 2.2: Income by tenure 1995-96

Tenure	Gross average weekly household income
Owner occupier	£465
LA tenants	£179
HA tenants	£179
Other tenants	£292
All tenures	£381

Adapted from Office for National Statistics, 1996, Family Spending 1995-96.

This data is supported by research carried out by MORI for the Housing Corporation, which revealed new facts on the gap between average incomes and the incomes of association tenants. The report quoted different data sources showing national average income at £298 compared to data on association tenant income of £128. In its commentary the Housing Corporation (1996) acknowledged 'associations are now housing the poorest and most vulnerable people in our society'.

However, not all home owners are rich nor are all social housing tenants poor. Table 2.3 shows the distribution of households among a range of income brackets.

Table Appendix 2.3: Percentage household distribution by tenure and income range

	Income range £ per week						
Tenure	<100	100-200	200-300	300-400	400-500	500-600	>600
Owner occupiers	11	19	18	16	11	9	17
LA tenants	48	34	11	4	1	0	0
HA tenants	45	33	12	6	2	1	1
PRS tenants	35	20	16	12	7	3	6
All tenures	22	22	16	13	9	7	12

Adapted from Table A8.10 in Green et al (1997): *Housing in England 1995/96*: HMSO

There are poor owner occupiers as well as poor households in the social rented sector. The trend, however, is towards growing poverty concentrated within the social rented sector.

As with housing and poverty, there is an inter-relationship between health and income. The current Government, unlike the previous Conservative Administration, has acknowledged the links between poverty, poor health and bad housing. Tessa Jowell, the Minister for Public Health, in July 1997 commented that:

> *"Poverty, unemployment, bad housing, social isolation, pollution, ethnic minority status, and gender have for too long been regarded as peripheral to health policy."*

The links between housing standards, tenure and homelessness with health were, however, strongly brought out as far back as 1980 in the Black Report. The relationship is a straight forward intuitive one. Those with no housing have the highest illness and mortality rates. These rates decline as one moves from local authority to private rented and finally to owner occupation.

Table 2.4 shows how death rates compare with three indicators of a person's social position – tenure, social class, and education. It uses the Standard Mortality Ratio, which measures actual deaths as a percentage of expected deaths, for men aged 15-64, for the period 1971-1981. The lower the number, the longer people live.

Table Appendix 2.4: Mortality differences by socio economic position

Indicator of Social position		Standardised Mortality Rate
Housing Tenure	Owner occupation	85
	Private rented	108
	Local authority	117
Social Class	I	67
	II	77
	IINM	105
	IIIM	96
	IV	125
	V	189
Education Qualification	Degree	51
	A level	87
	None	104

Source: Goldblatt P (1990)

This statistical relationship for the adult population shown in the table is mirrored by evidence on child deaths. Research confirms that stillbirths rates and infant death rates are higher among babies born to private tenants compared with those born to owner occupiers (Macfarlane and Mugford, 1989).

More generally, geographical inequalities in health have been rising over the last decades. Although absolute mortality rates for all groups have fallen since the 1950s, the gap between people living in different areas has widened. People under 65 living in the worst areas were almost twice as likely to die in 1990-92 than those in the best (Dorling, 1997). And the worst areas are also where the indicators of poverty are greatest.

At a local level, the relationship between poor health and tenure is equally striking. Marian Keogh, speaking at the CIH Annual Conference in 1997, pointed out how the Greater Easterhouse area of Glasgow (which consists of a number of large peripheral council estates) had an unenviable health record. Greater Easterhouse in relation to Glasgow has:

- twice the Glasgow rate of low birthweight;
- half the rate of breast feeding;
- 50% more mothers and fathers who smoke; and
- 50% more mothers aged under 20 years.

The evidence from those experiencing the highest level of housing poverty, homelessness, is compelling. Statistics from street homelessness deaths reveal life expectancy is considerably shortened through street life; 47 years compared to 73 years for men in the UK (Keyes and Kennedy, 1992).

In relation to links between housing, education and poverty, Power et al (1995) investigated the issue in relation to homeless people. The research identified the impact of temporary accommodation, the lack of thought to the transition between schools, and emotional distress for parents and children. Indeed as the Chartered Institute of Housing (1995) pointed out in 'all of us depend on suitable and reasonable housing in order to take full advantage of educational opportunities'.

Yet over 180,000 people live in non-permanent housing. Moreover in the social rented sector, there has been an increase in household mobility linked to the decline in the number of stable communities – 25% of local authority tenants have moved in the last two years. Children in lower socio economic households perform less well at all age groups, and the gap between them grows rather than diminishes during their time in state education.

In relation to diet, health and poverty, research reveals a number of interesting aspects of purchasing habits and budget priorities and coping strategies (Dobson et al, 1994) . There is a clear difference in purchasing habits between benefit and low income households and the general population, in relation to:

- shops used;
- frequency of shopping; and
- items purchased.

Lower income householders spend more time shopping, comparing prices between shops. They shop more often, buying as things are needed, or to secure the best price. In terms of the items purchased there was a preference for items which all members of the family are known to eat, and away from items that may go off and be wasted, like fresh fruit and vegetables. In practice this encouraged the food purchaser to buy items which their partner and particularly their children enjoy. Food expenditure was often the flexible part of the household budget. Larger than expected bills or other unforeseen costs eat into the food budget. However, rather than children or partners going without, or sharing the burden, it was usually the food purchaser who went without.

Low income householders spend a higher proportion of their household income on food. According to the Government's Family Expenditure Survey, the poorest 10% of the population spend 25% of their income on food, compared with 15% for the richest 10%. Save the Children pointed out in April 1997 that women living in low income families sacrificed their own food needs for their children, but even so could not provide them with a healthy diet (Owens, 1997). This study was based on a survey of 45 women living on incomes below 50% of national average, on five deprived council estates in Belfast, Coventry, Glasgow, Sunderland and Wandsworth where unemployment, for example, ranged from over 25% to nearly 55%. The study also highlighted that many factors contributed to this situation of a lack of a healthy diet including:

- poorly stocked local shops;
- lack of access to affordable transport including low levels of car ownership; and
- inadequate benefit levels.

❑ Unequal impact of poverty

The previous section has illustrated how poverty, poor health and tenure are associated with social class. However, there are other dimensions to inequality in terms of the impact of poverty including gender, ethnicity, age and disability. All of these dimensions overlap with aspects of housing inequalities, and will affect the development of anti-poverty strategies.

In relation to **gender**, in 1992, 5.4 million women (and 4.2. million men) were living in poverty as defined by being on or below income support levels (Oppenheim and Harker 1996). And, over 40% of female heads of household are in the social rented sector compared to just over 20% of male heads of household.

In relation to **ethnicity** and poverty, unemployment rates are a useful proxy indicator. The average unemployment rate in 1994/95 was over 40% for the

Bangladeshi population and 30% for Black Africans compared to 8% for the white population (Walker and Walker, 1997). In relation to housing opportunities, Skellington (1996) points out that while Pakistani/Bangladeshi households had high levels of owner occupation they also experienced high levels of unfitness and overcrowding.

Risk of poverty is also closely associated with **age**. The young, especially children, and the elderly are particularly vulnerable, as the following illustrate:

- According to the Child Poverty Action Group retired households were dependent on social security benefits for an average of 50% of their household income in 1994/95 compared to 13% for all households (Oppenheim and Harker, 1996). And between 1979 and the early 1990s the risk of poverty tripled for couples with children but only doubled for couples without.
- *The Guardian* pointed out in April 1997 that 'more children were living in poverty in the UK than in any other European Union country' (*The Guardian*, 28th April 1997, p 1). Over 30% of children were affected compared, for example, to 15% in the Netherlands and only 5% in Denmark.
- Because of poverty, 10% of children in the UK go without three or more things which the majority of parents believe are necessary (Middleton et al, 1997).
- In the Greater Easterhouse area of Glasgow, 65% of children get free school meals and over 80% get clothing grants. (Marion Keogh at the CIH 1997 Annual Conference.)

In relation to **disability**, research shows that nearly 50% of disabled adults are living in poverty (Oppenheim and Harker, 1996). Homelessness has increased among disabled people at double the rate for other groups during the 1980s and early 1990s. As about 65% of disabled people are elderly, they are also likely to be at risk of experiencing poor housing conditions.

❑ Geographical inequality

The scale and nature of poverty depends on where you live (Oppenheim and Harker, 1996). This can be examined in terms of regions, local areas and types of areas. In England in relation to the former, the proportion of primary school children receiving free school meals (which is often used as a proxy measure for poverty) in 1994 varied from 14% in East Anglia to nearly 25% in the North as against a national average of 19%. In the other parts of the UK, the figures were 23% for Scotland, 25% for Wales and 30% for N Ireland.

In relation to housing and anti-poverty initiatives, John Ward, Chairman of Scottish Homes commented at the CIH Scottish Branch Conference in Spring 1997 on the overlap between indicators of deprivation including crime, poor health, low skill levels and alcohol and drug abuse. Using an indicator such as lone parents (which he argued was a sign of community breakdown) 13 out of the 20 constituencies with highest proportion of lone parents were in Scotland and that 5 out of the top 6 were in Glasgow. These constituencies coincided with the large peripheral housing estates which exhibited high levels of poverty and social exclusion using other indicators.

Poverty and social exclusion are not just an urban issue of problem estates and older inner areas. Poverty exists in rural areas but is often hidden and ignored. Some of the commonly used indicators of poverty are implicitly urban-orientated, e.g. low levels of car-ownership and unemployment rates. But in rural areas, car-ownership is essential because of the dispersed public and private services combined with the lack of public transport. Similarly, unemployment rates are not particularly useful, as the issue in rural areas is often one of low paid, part-time or seasonal jobs. Cloke et al (1994) found poverty affecting nearly 25% of households in 12 case studies in rural areas. The highest figure was nearly 40% in part of rural Nottinghamshire.

■ References and further reading

Abel-Smith B and Townsend P (1965): *The Poor and the Poorest*: London, Bell and Sons

Alcock P (1993): *Understanding Poverty*: London, Macmillan

Alcock P et al (1995): *Combating Local Poverty*: Luton, LGMB

Black Report (1980): *Inequalities in Health*: London, DHSS

Bradshaw J (1993): *Household Budgets and Living Standards*: York, JRF

Clapham D et al (1996): *Citizenship and Housing – Shaping the Debate*: Coventry, CIH

Cloke P et al (1994): *Lifestyles in Rural England*: Salisbury, Rural Development Commission

Dennis N (1997): The Invention of Permanent Poverty: *Choices in Welfare* No 34: London, IEA

Dobson B et al (1994): *Diet, Choice and Poverty*: London and York, Family Policy Studies Centre and JRF

Dorling D (1997): *Death in Britain – How Local Mortality Rates have Changed – 1950s to 1990s*: York, Joseph Rowntree Foundation and York Publishing Services

Etzioni A (1995): *The Spirit of Community*: London, Fontana Press

Etzioni A (1997): *The New Golden Rule – Community and Morality in a Democratic Society*: London, Profile Books

Goldblatt P (1990): Mortality and Alternative Social Classifications. In Goldblatt P: *Mortality and Social Organisation – Longitudinal Studies 1971-1981*: London, OPCS

Hatchett W (1996): Housing – Local Strategies can ensure Dignity of Full Citizenship: *Housing*, July / August, p13

Housing Corporation (1996): *Housing Corporation News*: London, Housing Corporation, September

Hutton W (1995): *The State We're In*: London, Jonathan Cape

Hutton W (1997a): *The State to Come*: London, Vintage Press

Hutton W (1997b): Stakeholding and its Critics: *Choice in Welfare* No 36: London, IEA

Hutton W (1997c): New Labour, New Levers: *Housing*, May, pp 24-25

Joseph Rowntree Foundation (1995): *Inquiry into Income and Wealth – Volumes I and II*: York, JRF

Keyes S and Kennedy M (1992): *Sick to Death of Homelessness*: London, Crisis

Macfarlane A and Mugford M (1989): *Birth Counts – Statistics of Pregnancy and Childbirth*: London, OPCS

Middleton S et al (1997): *Small Fortunes – Spending on Children, Childhood Poverty and Parental Sacrifice*: York, Joseph Rowntree Foundation and York Publishing Services

Murray C (1996): Charles Murray and the Underclass – The Developing Debate: *Choice in Welfare* No 33: London, IEA

Oppenheim C and Harker L (1996): *Poverty – The Facts*: London, Child Poverty Action Group, 3rd Revised Edition

Owens B (1997): *Out of the Frying Pan – The True Costs of Feeding a Family on a Low Income*: London, Save the Children

Page D (1994): *Developing Communities*: York, JRF

Page D (1993): *Building for Communities*: York, JRF

Power A and Tunstall R (1997): *Dangerous Disorder – Riots and Violent Disturbances in 13 Areas of Britain in 1991-1992*: York, Joseph Rowntree Foundation and York Publishing Services

Power S et al (1995): *No Place to Learn*: London, Shelter

Putnam D (1992): *Making Democracy Work*: Princeton NJ, Princeton University Press

Report of the Commission on Social Justice [Borrie Commission] (1994): *Social Justice – Strategies for National Renewal*: London, Vintage Press

Roll J (1993): *Understanding Poverty – A Guide to the Concepts and Measures*: London, Family Policy Studies Centre, Occasional Paper No 15

Skellington R (1996): *'Race' in Britain Today*: London, Sage (2nd Edition)

Townsend P (1996): *A Poor Future*: London, Lemos and Crane

Walker A and Walker C (Eds) (1997): *Britain Divided*: London, CPAG

Willis J (1991): Line of Action on Poverty: *Local Government Chronicle*, 18th October

APPENDIX 3

DEFINING AND MEASURING POVERTY

❑ Introduction

The early chapters and appendices illustrate that poverty is a complex and bewildering term. Defining poverty and associated terminology is a necessary and important task so as to ensure that organisations and individuals are discussing the same phenomenon. It is equally important that measures of poverty are clarified, as a wide range of quantitative indicators are used.

Readers should also note that Appendix 4 provides a glossary of some of the relevant terminology.

❑ Defining poverty

A wide range of terminology is used in defining poverty. A general definition is that poverty is a term which describes the state of an individual or group where there is a lack of resources which affect well-being.

The more specific definition which has been adopted in this guide is that of the European Council of Ministers (1984):

> *"... persons, families and groups of persons whose resources (material, cultural, social) are so limited as to exclude them from the minimum acceptable way of life in the Member State in which they live."*

Of course, this statement begs many questions such as – what is the minimum acceptable way of life and how can it be quantified? and – what is meant by terms such as social resources? It is, therefore, important to identify the various detailed and specific terms which have been used to answer these types of questions.

Absolute Poverty

(also referred to as *Primary Poverty*)

Usually this refers to basic levels of food, clothing and shelter without which people would die, i.e. a lack of basic resources which may result in a life threatening situation.

Cycle of Deprivation

(also referred to as *Transmitted Deprivation*)

This refers to the idea that poverty and deprivation may be transferred across generations by the family or by the wider community. It is now often used in conjunction with the concept of underclass (see below).

Decency Threshold

More accurately, this is the Council of Europe's decency threshold and focuses on the level of earnings for those in work. It is interpreted as 68% of average earnings.

Deprivation

This term tends to be used interchangeably with poverty. Many specific forms of deprivation are used in the literature including:

- physical deprivation which equates with lack of material resources such as adequate food and shelter;
- basic deprivation consisting of the lack of items such as food; and
- secondary deprivation consisting of the lack of items such as a car, telephone or being able to participate in the wider community.

New Poverty

This term has become increasingly used since the end of the 1980s in European Union circles to describe new groups of people who are becoming poor. Traditionally, it was assumed that the poor comprised mainly, for example, the elderly, the unemployed and lone parent households. There is now a growing appreciation that other groups are affected such as low paid workers.

Objective Definition of Poverty

This refers to approaches which are based on academic/expert definitions of poverty and can be contrasted with subjective approaches, i.e. whether a person, family or group feel that they are poor.

Participation Standard

(or *Deprivation Standard*)

This is often associated with social exclusion and refers to the lack of ability of individuals, households and groups to participate in activities which are generally regarded by society as customary, e.g. being able to take an annual holiday away from home.

Poverty Trap

(or *Benefit Trap*)
This is associated with high marginal tax rates. It refers to a situation where a large proportion of any extra earned income is lost due to a combination of taxes and the withdrawal of means tested benefits.

Relative Poverty

Unlike absolute poverty, this refers to a comparison between individuals, households and groups and some norm which may be defined locally, nationally or internationally. Relative poverty is time and location specific.

Relative Deprivation

This term illustrates the complexity and confusion over definitions. One approach is to define relative deprivation as where people cannot participate in the 'normal' activities of society as defined by experts – it is thus closely linked to the 'participation standard'. A different approach is to use this term in a subjective sense as to whether people feel deprived relative to other people.

Social Exclusion

This is closely associated with the European Union Council of Ministers' approach – see above. It has become the accepted official EU definition. It is usually contrasted with financial and monetary definitions of poverty. Different forms of exclusion are often identified including economic exclusion and civic exclusion as well as social exclusion.

Underclass

This also is an extremely contentious term. It is often used to mean a group of people who are cut off from the rest of society in terms of geographical locality, economic circumstances and by their behaviour. It is also often used especially in the USA to refer to minority ethnic groups. It is important, however, to appreciate that the original use of the term related to economic exclusion.

❑ Measuring poverty

As with the definitions of poverty, there are a wide range of measures of poverty. They, nevertheless, can be grouped into a number of categories. It is important to appreciate that most measures of poverty focus on quantitative/

statistical data. There have been few successful and widely accepted measures that build on qualitative definitions such as social exclusion.

■ Official estimates

Britain, unlike other countries such as the USA, does not have an official poverty line. Nevertheless, the Government publishes official statistics which are frequently referred to as the 'official poverty figures'. The main source of information is the Government's annual Family Expenditure Survey (FES). From this data, the Government produced statistics on 'low income families' until the mid 1980s and has subsequently published data on 'households below average incomes'. The data on low income families is now published independent of Government by the House of Commons Social Security Committee.

Both sets of data underestimate the scale of poverty as, for instance, the FES does not include homeless people.

It is up to individual organisations how they interpret the poverty line in both sets of statistics – Low Income Families (LIF) and Households Below Average Incomes (HBAI).

The Child Poverty Action Group uses the following two poverty lines:

- LIF – As the data shows the number of people living on or below the supplementary benefit/income support level, this is used as a proxy for the poverty line; and
- HBAI – the poverty line is defined as 50% of average incomes after housing costs and adjusted for family size.

The results for the LIF poverty line show that in 1979 14% of the population were living on or below the supplementary benefit level while in 1992 nearly 25% of the population were living on or below income support level.

The results for the HBAI poverty line show that in 1979 less than 10% of the population were living below 50% of average incomes after housing costs, while in 1993/94 the figure had risen to 24% of the population.

Each of these approaches has its own strengths and weaknesses – the HBAI figure is a relative-based measure, while the LIF data relates to the Government's view of what is an acceptable minimum level of income. The key point is that, whichever measure is used, there has been a significant rise in the levels of poverty over the last two decades.

European Union measures of poverty

The threshold used by the European Union is individual expenditure below 50% of national equalised average. For Britain, the information is obtained from the Family Expenditure Survey, while for other countries a diverse range of sources are used. It is therefore rather difficult to compare all EU countries.

The evidence from the late 1980s and early 1990s shows that:

- countries in Southern Europe such as Portugal, Italy and Greece have the highest levels of poverty – 26.5%, 22.0% and 20.8% respectively;
- the UK figure was 17%; and
- countries such as the Netherlands and Belgium have much lower rates of poverty – 6.2% and 7.5% respectively.

Breadline Britain

This approach is associated with two surveys conducted for television programmes in 1983 and 1990. A further survey is due for publication in the late 1990s. Interviewees were asked what they thought were necessities that all people should be able to afford from a list drawn up by experts. Those that were chosen by at least 50% of the sample were classed as necessities. Over 30 items fell into this category including a damp free home through to an outing for children once per week. All those people who lacked three or more of these necessities were defined as poor.

In 1990, 11 million people (or 20% of households) were poor according to this definition compared to 7.5 million in 1983.

Budget standards

The Family Budget Unit at the University of York has drawn up a 'modest but adequate budget standard' for different family types drawing on a range of information including advice from experts and consumer groups, as well as analysing expenditure data.

This type of approach has a long pedigree and is also referred to as a 'basket of goods' approach. It was used by Rowntree in his studies on poverty during the first half of this Century. The official poverty line in the USA is also based on the principles behind this type of system.

In the Family Budget Unit approach, items are included if more than half the population have them or they are regarded as necessities by the general public. They include, for instance, one week's annual holiday in the UK but not a holiday abroad.

It is argued that this type of measure most nearly fits the definition of social exclusion, as the modest but adequate budget standard represents a level of income which allows people to participate fully in society.

Finally, if the poverty line definitions used in conjunction with LIF and HABI are compared with the modest but adequate budget, it suggests that the former significantly underestimates the scale of poverty in this country:

- for a couple with two young children, only 46% of a modest but adequate budget is met by income support; and
- for a couple with two small children, only 66% of a modest but adequate budget is met by 50% of average income.

The figures for other household types such as single people and couples without children suggest an even greater under estimation of poverty and social exclusion.

Appendix 4

Glossary

Anti-Poverty Strategy is defined by the Local Government Anti-Poverty Unit as 'a corporate strategy whereby scarce resources can be more effectively directed towards poor people, services made more accessible to them and greater control over their own living standards made possible for them'.

Citizenship: There are many definitions of citizenship including the notion that it comprises of three sets of rights – civil rights such as free speech, political rights such as the ability to participate in the exercise of political power, and social rights such as entitlements to welfare.

Communitarianism: This concept is now closely associated with the writings of an American author, Amitai Etzioni. He argues that rights as part of citizenship need to be considered in relation to a requirement to 'shore up our moral responsibilities', i.e. rights and responsibilities must be in balance in order to create sustainable communities.

Housing Plus is usually defined as the added value that housing organisations bring through their business and service functions, social roles and links to the local communities in tackling aspects of, for instance, poverty and social exclusion.

Poverty is defined in more detail in the previous appendix. It is a term which describes the state of an individual, family or group where there is a lack of resources which significantly affects well-being.

Social Capital refers to the need for society to develop clusters and dense networks of links between individuals and groups leading to a mutuality of interests and trust. It is argued by writers, such as Robert Puttnam, that social capital is as important as physical capital/infrastructure and intellectual capital in creating a well functioning society.

Social Cohesion and **Social Integration** are terms used to express what is required to be done to avoid and overcome social exclusion (see Appendix 3). They focus on aspects such as recreating a fairer and more equal society so avoiding the extremes of wealth and poverty as described in, for example, Douglas Massey's *Age of Extremes*.

Stakeholder Society: Will Hutton argues that there is a need to create a stakeholder society as a means of expressing national solidarity. It involves an alternative way forward compared to socialist collectivism and market individualism. It consists of a democratically accountable welfare state involving providers, funders and users collaborating together.

APPENDIX 5

RULES OF LETS

Suggested Rules of LETS (Devised by LETSlink UK)

a) .... LETS is a non profit membership club. It is organised by the .... LETS Management Committee, who act on behalf of members.

b) .... LETS provides an information service through which members can exchange goods and services, and maintains a central account of that exchange for the benefit of members.

c) Members agree to .... LETS holding their details on computer, and is bound by the Data Protection Act. This information will be distributed to members relevant to the purposes of exchange.

d) Members may give or receive from one another credit in the .... LETS units, called .... The .... units are recorded centrally on the .... LETS accounts. The .... is considered to represent a hour's worth of labour.

e) Only the account holder can authorise the transfer of units from their account to that of another (except for service charges, which may be transferred by the accountant to the system's administration account).

f) No interest is charged on accounts. The management is authorised to charge joining and renewal fees, set by the Management Committee. Both are set at a cost of service basis.

g) All accounts start at zero. Members are not obliged to have credit in their account before issuing another member with credit, subject to a limit set by the Management Committee.

h) No money is deposited with or issued from the LETS account. Members may engage in any transaction entirely in LETS units, or on a part cash basis, but only LETS units are recorded on the LETS account.

i) No one is obliged to accept any particular invitation to trade or to engage in any transaction with another member. On leaving .... LETS, however, members are obliged to balance their accounts.

j) Any member is entitled to know the balance and turnover of another members account. To ensure accountability the Management Committee may decide to publish the balance and turnover from time to time.

k) .... LETS gives no warranty or undertaking as to the value, condition or quality of services or item offered. Members should seek to determine for themselves the quality or standard of workmanship offered before agreeing a purchase. .... LETS publishes a directory of services available, but cannot be held responsible for the quality of goods or services on offer.

l) Members are individually responsible for their own tax liabilities and returns. They are also responsible for reviewing the effect on other incomes and benefits. .... LETS has no liability for tax or benefits of participants, and has no obligation or liability to report to the tax or benefit offices, or collect taxes or other payments on their behalf.

m) The .... LETS administrator may decline to record an account or directory entry considered inappropriate for legal or other reasons.

n) Members have the right to attend any meeting of the Management Committee, as an observer.

o) The Management Committee, which consists of .... members is elected annually by all members through a ballot at the AGM. All members will be invited to the AGM. Any member has the right to stand for election to the Management Committee.

p) The Management Committee will appoint a Chair who will Chair the Management Committee. It will also appoint an Arbitration Officer, who will arbitrate in disputes between members. The Arbitration Officer will not be a member of the Management Committee, but will be a member of the .... LETS.

q) The Management Committee may deny membership to any applicant without reason. The Management Committee may interview a member to gain explanation to activities which it considers are not in the interests of .... LETS. The Management Committee may suspend a member, or remove members from the system. In such cases there is a right of appeal to the Arbitration Officer.

r) Members agree to abide by the conditions of these rules and those embodied in the .... LETS constitution.

APPENDIX 6

USEFUL CONTACTS

❑ Introduction

Readers requiring further information on the issues discussed in each of the chapters are urged to follow up the references in the 'Guides to Further Reading' at the end of each of the chapters.

Contact points for information on specific projects and strategies are listed below and were correct as at summer 1997. They have been organised on a topic basis.

❑ Housing and anti-poverty strategies

■ General information on local authority anti-poverty strategies

Adrian Harvey
Local Government Anti-Poverty Unit
Layden House
76-78 Turnmill Street
London EC1M 5QU

■ Examples of local authority anti-poverty strategies including research and poverty profiles

Sheila Rushforth
Community Safety and Anti-Poverty
Policy Division
Chief Executive's Department
Birmingham City Council
The Council House
Victoria Square
Birmingham B1 1BB

Tim Marren
Anti-Poverty Officer
Coventry City Council
Council House
Coventry CV1 5RT

Marketing Unit
Portsmouth City Council
Civic Offices
Guildhall Square
Portsmouth PO1 2BC

Tudor Owen
Community Services Division
Stockport MBC
Ponsonby House
Edward Street
Stockport SK1 3PT

■ Examples of housing association anti-poverty strategies

Moat Housing Group
St John's House
Suffolk Way
Sevenoaks
Kent
TN13 1TG

❑ Research on social policy, poverty and housing policy

Child Poverty Action Group
1-5 Bath Street
London EC1V 9PY

Joseph Rowntree Foundation
The Homestead
40 Water End
York YO3 6LP

❑ Overviews of core housing activities and anti-poverty projects

Good Practice Unit
Chartered Institute of Housing
Octavia House
Westwood Way
Coventry CV4 8JP

Jon Passmore
Taff Housing Association
43 Lower Cathedral Road
Cardiff CF1 8LW

Priority Estates Project
3rd Floor City Point
701 Chester Road
Manchester M32 0RW

❑ Examples of core housing activities and anti-poverty projects

■ Benefit advice

Bill Irvine
Head of Information, Advice and Advocacy services
Housing Services
South Lanarkshire Council
Brandon Gate
1 Leechlee Road
Hamilton ML3 0XB

■ Debt recovery

Trish McCue
Social Strategy Co-ordinator
Chief Executive's Department
Leicester City Council
New Walk Centre
Leicester LE1 6ZG

■ Energy efficiency

National Energy Advice
St Andrew's House
90-92 Pilgrim Street
Newcastle-upon-Tyne NE1 6SG

Hastoe Housing Association
Harlequin House
7 High Street
Teddington TW11 8EL

■ Furniture schemes

Glyn Meacher
City of Salford Housing Services
Ordsall Neighbourhood Office
2 Robert Hall Street
Ordsall
Salford M5 3 LT

Bob Kilpatrick
Group Welfare Benefits Unit
Notting Hill Housing Trust
Grove House
27 Hammersmith Grove
London W16 0JL

■ Hardship Funds

Richard Newcombe
Cambridge Housing Society
1A Fortescue Road
Cambridge

■ Home contents insurance

Graham Marsh
North British Housing Association – Manchester
7th Floor Paragon House
48 Seymour Grove
Old Trafford
Manchester M16 0LN

■ Money management advice

Cheryl Daniels
Business Debtline
Birmingham Settlement
318 Summer Lane
Birmingham B19 3RL

■ Rents

Dorcas Ward
The Guinness Trust
17 Mendy Street
High Wycombe
Bucks HP11 2NZ

■ Rent deposit schemes

Simon Prendergast
Crisis
1st Floor Challenger House
42 Alder Street
London E1 1EE

❑ Overviews of non-core housing activities and anti-poverty projects

Marian Keogh
Greater Easterhouse Initiative
1200 Westerhouse Road
Easterhouse
Glasgow G34 9HZ

New Economics Foundation
1st Floor Vine Court
112-116 Whitechapel Road
London E1 1JE

People for Action 2001
1 Causeway
Blackheath
West Midlands B65 8AA

❑ Examples of non-core housing activities and anti-poverty projects

■ Community self-build

Anna McGettigan
Community Self-Build Agency
Finsbury Business Centre
40 Bowling Green Lane
London EC1R 0NE

■ Credit Unions

Ken Dunn
Sheffield Credit Union Development Agency
Aizlewood's Mill
Nursery Street
Sheffield S3 8GG

■ Employment

Liz Shephard
Letslink UK
61 Woodcock Road
Warminster
Wiltshire BA12 9DH

Shokoya Eleshin Construction Ltd
108 Tower Street
Century Building
Brunswick Business Park
Sefton Street
Liverpool L3 4BJ

■ Health

Valerie Cotter
Sheffield Health
Fulwood House
5 Old Fulwood Road
Sheffield S10 3TG

■ Training

Foyers:
Tim Clarke
Leicester Housing Association
Nottingham Area Office
4 Layton Avenue
Mansfield NG18 5PL

Rushden Renovate:
Nicola Yates
East Northamptonshire District Council
Cedar Drive
Thrapston
Northamptonshire NN14 4LZ

❑ Funding

■ Social investment agencies

Aston Reinvestment Trust
The Rectory
3 Tower Street
Birmingham B19 3UY

■ Use of National Lottery funding

Harry Perry
Leicester Newarke Housing Association
17 Millstone Lane
Castle Park
Leicester LE1 5JN